Advertising Superpowers.
Tricks For Creating Great Ads.
Santiago Cosme

Adapted into English by Psembi Kinstan.
Illustrated by Neil Johnston.

Copyright © 2017 Santiago Cosme
All rights reserved.

Contents

Introduction	12
01. Put some effort in and you'll be ok.	18
02. Brainstorming is for those who ask loads of questions.	26
03. Don't judge ideas too quickly.	36
04. Every idea has its moment.	44
05. The answer is one millimeter away.	58
06. Have you ever read the brief?	64
07. Walls are uninspiring.	72
08. If you like it, take it.	78
09. Accept your brand.	88
10. Get recognised.	96
11. Use the name of your brand.	102
12. The power of saying yes.	110
13. The art of…	118
14. Create conflict whatever it takes.	126
15. Without tension, you have nothing.	138
16. Go literal, not lateral.	152
17. Donate your mum.	160
18. Pressure helps.	170
19. Simply simplify.	178
20. Make them curious, show a benefit, or stand out.	186
21. Don't believe in yourself, but believe in your idea.	196
22. Don't compete, just win.	202
23. No one tests your idea better than you.	208
24. You're cupid, stupid.	214
25. Make the headlines with your headlines.	220
26. The end.	228
Glossary	237
Credits	241

ADVERTISING SUPERPOWERS

Who is SANTIAGO COSME?

About the author

If I follow the most conventional way of introducing yourself, I should mention that I teach creativity in Miami Ad School, and when allowed to, I do speaking engagements in places such as Google, Leroy Merlin, Indra, ESIC Business School, University of Malaga, etc...

As a creative, I have worked for short periods in some well-known agencies such as Grey New York, Mother London, Remo Madrid, Buzzman Paris and Young & Rubicam Prague. I have worked for brands such as Coca-Cola, Harley-Davidson, Doctors Without Borders, Hyundai, Mitsubishi, Tipp-Ex or Jameson Whiskey. Some of my work has also been awarded in Cannes, D&AD, One Show, Eurobest, Golden Drum, and even AMPE (Yes, no one knows it).

But, in reality, to say all this is to say nothing. Many people can say they have worked in large agencies, and many others can pump their chest and go through their endless list of advertising awards (with more than 800 advertising festivals a year, whoever has not won any is probably in the wrong industry or the wrong agency).

Instead of this typical Wikipedia non-sense. I'd rather tell you who I was 10/20 years ago, and so you'll get a better idea of what kind of person I am.

In 1993, a time when people still called me Santi, I was a lost young man who stopped studying as soon as he finished high school. It was a massive blow to my mother who had always dreamt of seeing her son grow up to become someone respectable and go to La Sorbonne University in Paris.

Instead, I broke her heart and spent my "college years" doing almost nothing. I worked as a pizza delivery man and had my first contact with advertising distributing leaflets in my city's mailboxes. Without any studies or any work training, my future did not look too bright. That's why nobody was surprised when I started working in construction. My colleagues were good people, without a doubt, but this was not the situation I had dreamt of as a child. So after three years, I packed my bags and returned to Paris (the city where I was born) with only one goal: a new beginning. I was 23 years old.

As soon as I arrived in France they offered me a job as "Cast Member" in Euro Disney, Paris. Considering my recent work experience, the idea of working in a place that makes people dream seemed like a good start.

Unfortunately, things did not start as well as I expected. A mistake on the part of the human resources department meant that, at least for a while, I would not be working in any of the magnificent and amusing attractions. No, I would need to clean the public restrooms to start with. To this day, I still do not know what I liked the most about that brief period of my life: whether to clean toilets used by an average of 40,000 people a day, or sweep off horse manure from the park. Either way, I felt that I would soon be occupying my rightful place.

And I did! About 100 pounds of horse manure later, I became Tigger! Loved by all the children, embraced by all the mothers and adored by a good number of young ladies. Yes, getting dressed as Tigger makes you more adorable.

But all those displays of affection and love did not blind me. I knew there was not much future in the land of Disney. So, after almost a year there, I moved to the UK to learn English. First, I lived in Dublin, but I really did not feel in connection with that city, Molly Malone, or the Paddies. After a few months, I moved to London, where I would spend the next 8 years of my life.

Every person who goes to London without a good command of English ends up working in a hotel, a pub or a store like Zara or Mango. In my case, I was given a job in a hotel as a bellboy first and then as a hotel concierge. Unlike advertising, where you are encouraged to grow a beard and have the most varied hairstyles, at the hotel I was forced to keep my hair short, to shave every day, and to put on a penguin coat with matching shoes.

After a few years in the world of hospitality, I ended up in one of the best hotels in the world: the Dorchester. For a while, it was fun to be surrounded by famous people and to get to know things about them that not even gossipy newspaper could ever dream to know. These are some of the highlights of my days at the Dorchester: shaking hands with Nelson Mandela, buying socks for Barbra Streisand's dog, posing for Paris Hilton, organizing a world trip for Anthony Hopkins and his wife, and of course the huge savings I made with all the commissions and tips.

In fact, I saved so much money, that after a couple of years there, I thought it was time to settle in and buy a flat. I wasn't really passionate about working in the hospitality industry, but at the age of 30, it felt like the right thing to do. However, life had other plans for me, and it made me aware of them in the morning of September 15th, 2008. That day Lehman Brothers collapsed. Within an hour my dreams of buying a house in London would vanish. The bank who was supposed to give me a mortgage called me, and said with the most soulless tone "The mortgage is off."

For me, these were not just some news, it was a life sign. I understood that if I ever had the opportunity to do something that I liked, it was now or never. The next day, I gave my resignation letter to my boss of the last 6 years, I left my apartment, I said goodbye to everyone and I moved back to Madrid to study advertising in Miami Ad School. I was almost 32, and I had more uncertainty before me that the collapse of Lehman Brothers could ever dream to create.

This second "new beginning" was tough. I was the eldest and I also did not seem to be really good at coming up with ideas. "Everyone is creative" they say. Well, for a while, I felt that was totally untrue. During my first year in Miami Ad School, I seriously thought that having left my stable life in London had been one of the great mistakes of my life. As if having those thoughts in my mind was not enough, just when I needed more support, a teacher of Miami Ad School saw my advertising campaigns and said: "You want to work in New York, London or Paris? Well, good luck to you." Although his words were not exactly constructive and quite damaging, I continued to work as much as I had been doing. Little by little, advertising began to start making sense. I learned things from my classmates. I soaked up all the ads I could see until

I became a walking encyclopedia of advertising and I worked longer hours than anyone more often than not. Going home last was the only thing that made me feel like I was on the right track.

In the end, I did work in New York, London and Paris. I wasn't trying to be revengeful or contradict that teacher from Miami Ad School. It just happened that way.

Now, as I look back I feel like my efforts were not in vain. I got to be in the place I wanted in the world of advertising and if I am writing this book it is because I know that I have learned some things that deserve to be shared. Things that, I strongly believe, can help you create better campaigns.

Yes, ladies and gentlemen, that's how I ended up working in advertising. It is an unusual way, considering that most people have 15 years of experience when they turn 40, but I am convinced that times have changed. Degrees are becoming obsolete, and are no longer a reflection of what companies ask for. With attitude, desire and guts, you can catch up and do in five years what others haven't done in twenty. I know, because I did it. A proof is that many creatives do not even have a shortlist in Cannes despite having spent their lives working for different agencies. In 5 years, have accumulated more than 40 awards, including those damned Cannes Lions. If I could do it, you can do it.

Why and how did I write this book?

I wrote it for several reasons.

— **The first one is that advertising led me to a sort of temporary insanity and to a long battle with anxiety. With "Advertising Superpowers", I wanted to do something that would excite me and allow me to have fun again with this unusual industry.**

— **I wrote this book for the simple reason that I feel like it and nobody can forbid me. I want to write a book, I write it.**

— **I wrote it because, nowadays, it seems that any professional that wants to command some respect has to write a book to prove his worth.**

— **Finally, I also wrote it because after reading many books about advertising creativity, I felt that most falsely claim to teach how to come up with ideas. Most only share a bunch of marketing concepts that have little value when you are facing a white page.**

I wrote "Advertising Superpowers" because I felt that I could share things you didn't know. Tricks that I have used many times to get out of trouble, keep my Creative Director happy, and make some of my campaigns worthy of a Lion at Cannes.

~

INTRO.

INTRODUCTION

> God did not make me creative.

No, I got that "superpower" by myself. Okay, it's not a "superpower" but it's the closest thing to having one. It's like being a mixture of Mazinger Z and a ham croquette.

In fact, creativity is the skill that allows me to say Mazinger Z and ham croquette in the same sentence and no one will blink. It also allows me to do crazy stuff in any party and people almost always forgive me because: "he is a creative dude".

Yes, according to people, you are either creative or you are not. And if you are not, you can't do anything about it.

My name is Santiago Cosme and I am an advertising creative, or for most people just a "creative" guy, and I understand that there are only two reasons why you have started reading this book:

1. **The title has caught your attention.**
2. **You want to know once and for all if there is a formula to be creative.**

I will take the liberty of believing that you are here for both option 1 and option 2, and I will spare you the suspense: yes, there is a formula to be creative.

My bad. There are many formulas to be creative.

My purpose with "Advertising Superpowers" is to take a topic as intangible as advertising, dissect it and share the formulas, methods and tricks I have discovered through my years in agencies around the world. Hopefully, they will help in your day to day in the world of creative advertising.

No, you are not the only ones who wonder how to get good ideas. Therefore, I hope this book will help you as much as the tricks I share in each chapter have helped me. We can all become great publicists.

If you do not believe me take a look at my first print ad, I made back in 2009 when I landed in Miami Ad School Madrid. My first ad and it belongs in the advertising Hall of Shame (Image 01). An airplane with a smiley, a painful art direction, an incomprehensible concept and a logo bigger than the plane itself. Wherever you look, my first print ad is one of the great horrors of advertising. In fact, it was saved from such an honor because it never saw the light. Thanks God. Either way, if I was to be judged by it, I clearly did not seem like a person who had any future in the advertising business.

INTRODUCTION

Image 01

However, after a lot of effort and after having to ignore some "I know it all" creatives trying to convince me that I had absolutely no future, and maybe that I should find another job, I started learning, on my own, my way, with my tricks. In fact, I learned so much that a few years later, I went from making a print as painful to look at as the Spanair ad to making this print for Forbes, which was among the most awarded in 2017 (Image 02).

Anyway, I do not want to screw your head with my stories. In the end, the important thing is that you realize that I am not more creative than you, nor am I a huge talent. I am just a guy works a lot and who has learned that whatever you do, you can improve over time.

~

INTRODUCTION

Image 02

Chapter 1

Put some EFFoRT in and you'll be OK.

> "There's only one thing
> you can control: your effort."
> **Mark Cuban**

I might get rid of half the readers with what comes next, but I'm not here to tell you what you want to hear, but to tell you the truth, which is already a lot. So, there I go; and for those who decide to close the book after this chapter: Ciao! Sayonara! Laters!

Well, without detours, what I want to say is that after years spending an average of 12 hours a day thinking about ideas to help clients of all kinds, from bankers to makers of smelly ravioli or websites to find couples where you never find anyone worth it, I can assure you that the element that above all made it possible to find a great idea was without a doubt, the effort I put in looking for it.

Yes, I know. It's bad news. It means working hard, it means that there is no secret, that I am an impostor, another fake "salesman". A guy who talks about tricks and then slaps us in the face with the typical "Work hard if you want to see results". No, it's not like that. There are tricks. For real! There are! But none will work if it is not accompanied by a major effort on your part. It is what it is. Ideas do not fall from the sky. Only planes fall from the sky, stones from scaffoldings and shits from inopportune birds.

What? You don't believe me? Edison himself, one of the greatest inventors in history, said it. No, not that thing about inopportune birds, the thing about the importance of effort. Edison, who came to patent more than a thousand ideas in his life, clarified the secret of his own creativity:

"Genius is 1% inspiration, and 99% perspiration."

The problem is that our mechanism of self-defense against people who do things better than us is very simple. We attribute everything to fortune. For many and many more also, triumph is synonymous with luck, and failure synonymous with bad luck. We do not like to recognize the hard work of people who succeed. We do not want to see that success is simply the accumulation of all the tiny efforts that we make every day. We prefer to think that the one who gets the best ideas was simply born with a more creative mind and that there's nothing you can do about it.

Well, surprise surprise, this is actually the first lesson to draw from this book: yes, creativity is a skill that we are all born with. Being a skill, it means that we can all develop it. It's like holding a tennis racket. Anybody can do it, but those who work harder on the tennis court will become better tennis players.

So, let's stop claiming that people are simply talented when they do something much better than average and look at several examples of people who were praised for their "ginormous talent," but who actually worked a lot harder than the ordinary.

André Agassi
For those who do not know him, André Agassi was one of the most precocious players in the history of tennis. He entered the professional circuit like a whirlwind at the age of 17. With his blonde hair and his jeans shorts, all the teenagers fell in love with him (including my sister), and with his game he dazzled all the tennis fans. The press was as quick to label him for his rebellious style as for his prodigious talent. However, what many of those supposed experts did not know is that André Agassi had been forced in his childhood to hit an average of 3000 balls a day. He stood in front of a ball-throwing machine that he called "monster", under the dictatorial supervision of his father, who was convinced that if someone hit about 1 million balls a year, sooner or later, that player would be invincible. For a while, during his career, Agassi

became the invincible player his father had programmed for years. So, what really turned him into star? His supposed innate talent or an effort and sacrifice completely out of this world?

Paco de Lucía

We can find another example of early effort in the figure of the late Paco de Lucía, who filled concert halls around the world playing guitar. As Paco de Lucía once said: "I would lock myself up to play the guitar as a boy when my friends were playing in the neighborhood." Even many years later, he continued with that same discipline and dedication, and locked himself in a cellar for two years with another guitarist, Manolo Sanlúcar, to perfect the technique of "El picado". However, when asked about his enormous talent for music, he humbly preferred to answer what he believed to be the truth: "Anyone can become the best guitarist in the world. They just need to be willing to practice 14 hours a day."

Jim Carrey

No matter how hard you think, very few people look like they were born for humor as much as the comedian Jim Carrey. God had given him everything he needed to succeed: a uniquely elastic face, a wit and audacity rarely seen, and a totally non-existent sense of ridicule. When you see his films, his stage performances, his imitations of Clint Eastwood and his performances in galas such as the Oscars, it is impossible to imagine that this Canadian actor had to suffer resounding failures in his performances as a comedian in his early days. No, Jim Carrey could not live on his "talent". In fact, he had to work as a janitor to help his family and only when he could, he found time to devote himself to humor and getting booed. Luckily, he did not despair and his perseverance and hard work led him to continue polishing his technique and improve his artistic skills. After many years of effort, sweat and ducking tomatoes, Jim Carrey achieved the success we all know. Now, apart from being a reference in the world of comedy, he is a figure known for his speeches and motivating interviews. Above all, he is an example that effort and guts is more important than natural talent.

Well, my dear friends, advertising in general and creativity in particular, is not very different. You'll make less money than if you played tennis, you'll laugh less than you would with a comedy show and, truth be told, it only serves to interrupt people. But, beyond that, good advertising depends fundamentally on one factor: work, sweat, desire or effort. Call it what you want.

No, God did not make me creative, nor did he make you. God gave us the seed of creativity and to some the ability to strive and sacrifice ourselves to become good advertising creatives. So, if you are not willing to work more than your colleagues in this business, to spend hours thinking and polishing ideas when the others have gone home with their wives or husbands; If you do not take this with a point of obsession and madness, this business will not make you a rock star. You will be just another creative. There's nothing wrong in it, but is that what you really want?

If you are reading this book, I doubt it.

~

Chapter 2

BRAINSTORMING IS for THOSE who ASK LOADS of QUESTIONS.

Paul Samuelson

Asking questions is something innate. In fact, they say that children ask about 400 questions a day, no more no less. As we grow up, our thirst for knowledge is dissipating and we are asking less and less questions. The average for an adult is as low as 50 questions per day.

In the world of advertising, we are constantly solving problems through solutions that do not exist yet. That is, if I have to make a campaign for a soft drink brand and I want to communicate happiness, there is no answer that I can automatically generate and present to the client. Therefore, I am forced to think of something new that hopefully nobody has thought of and produced before.

To find solutions to the problems posed by the clients brief, we must do one thing only: ask questions, over and over again. But I do not mean to ask to see if someone has a solution to the brief but rather questions about people's behavior and the brand.

We must learn to ask questions that help us establish conclusive human behaviors that are familiar to everyone. For instance (first things that come to mind): we all know young people study in libraries for hours but then easily lose their focus; We all know that in Latin countries mothers show their love through food; we all know that if you step on a banana peel you are likely to trip over.

Once you have found a scenario that is relatable to the product you want to find ideas for, the only thing you need to do is introduce that product and see how it destabilizes the situation. I know this sounds really abstract so let's take a break to do an exercise together that will allow us to understand this process much better.

Brainstorming exercise
Think of a three prints campaign for an energy drink (Monster, Red Bull, Gatorade or whichever you prefer). Think about what that campaign would look like visually and what the concept would be. You have ten minutes. Yes, that's it. When you're done, please come back to the book.

(10 minutes later).

Hello again. How was it? Have you got a cool print campaign for that energy drink? If so, congratulations. You are a genius and you should write a book to enlighten the world about your creative speed. If not, think for a moment about how your creative process was. How was the internal conversation you had with yourself? Did you think of random things? Did you follow a structure? Most importantly, did you ask yourself many questions? If you didn't, I think you should read what comes next, because this is where I give away how I come up with ideas in its own personal and unique way (at least, that's what I want to believe).

(Drum Roll sound).

Let's say that among those energy drinks I choose Monster to do the same exercise. My first question will always be focused on knowing who consumes that product: "Who drinks Monster?". Logic will tell that young people do. So, I continue down that road. I keep asking questions, and I always look for a concise answer: in what situation would a young person drink Monster?

To have energy when doing sports.
To have energy during the exam period.
To have energy when you go out at night.

Once I have established a few possible situations I try to find what sticks more with the tone of the brand or the one I think is more fun. Studying seems boring and between sports and going out, I'm left with the latest.

So I keep asking:
"What do young people do when they go out?"

They dance.
They drink alcohol.
They flirt.

Since we are making an ad for an energy drink, showing people consuming alcohol would look contradictory, so I stick to flirting cause it's a lot more fun too.

With only three questions, I have established a "true" situation: when young people go out at night, they like to flirt. Good! Now, I introduce the product and start thinking about a visual for the print: what would a situation be like when a boy is hitting on girls and has 10 times more energy? Several visuals come to mind:

A boy surrounded by a crowd of women.
A boy walking down the street pursued by women.
The same boy shown 10 times on the print talking to 10 different girls.

That's it, I have it. 100%.
And the tagline comes out just as easily:

"Monster. 10 times more energy 10 times more possibilities."

In just over 3 minutes, I have been able to create a print, that might not be worth an award, but that makes perfect sense and does fit the brand. How did I do it? I asked simple questions and answered them really simply too. I established a real situation and I integrated the product to see what would happen with it. If I want to make a second or third print to go with it, I would simply return to the last two questions.

I would make a print based on "young people need energy when doing sports". The image would show the same players multiplied by ten around the pitch. I could do that or create an ad in the world of studying or I could stick the world of partying and have the guy flirt in one print, dance in another, etc…

Now, I already have an idea, but I want to continue exploring, to know how far I can go. At this point, I try to create a conflict by asking myself who does not drink Monster? Obviously, what comes to my mind is the elderly.

As an advertising guy, I know that when we see old people in ads, it's generally Grannies. So, I asked myself some questions like in the previous example: What do grannies like to do? They like to cook. For whom? Their grandchildren. Again, I have established a "true" situation: "Grannies love to cook for their grandchildren".

Like I did before, I ask myself: What would a situation be like when a granny cooks for her grandson and she has 10 times more energy? Several visuals come to mind. One of them is simply a visual of a table for 10 people but with a single chair where the grandson is sitting with a frightened look on his face. Monster.

But I want to get more prints, so I go back and ask myself again. What else do Grannies do for their grandchildren? They love to knit! What do they knit?

Jerseys
Scarves
Gloves

I pick scarves simply because my instinct tells me it is more fun. So, what would a situation be like when a granny has knit a scarf for her grandson and she has 10 times more energy? Several visuals come to mind:

A giant scarf that the grandmother gives to the grandson who looks scared/surprised.
The grandson wearing a gigantic scarf, which gets lost in the hallway of the house.
The grandson rolled up like a mummy with a giant scarf that does not let him move.

My gut feeling tells me that the last one is the right one. The print that should complete the series alongside the food table.

At this point, I could easily finish but I feel there is one more path to explore. Being an energy drink, I think: who must absolutely drink Monster and have energy because the life of others depends on it? I think about it and these are the first 3 answers that come to my mind:

A bus driver.
An airplane pilot.
A surgeon.

My instinct tells me to continue with a surgeon that seems to lead to a more interesting path. So, I keep asking questions. What types of surgeons are there?

A surgeon who works in the emergency room.
A sports surgeon.
A plastic surgeon.

Bingo! Plastic surgeon seems like a path full of possibilities that can lead to funny things which tone can be relatable to Monster energy drink. So, what would a situation be like when a plastic surgeon has not had Monster? Again, a lot of visuals come to my head. Some are horrendous, others are a little better. I'll share one of them: I imagine a man with two women's breasts and a simple tagline that says something like: Plastic surgeons need energy. Buy Monster.

This is not a great ad by any means, but the process does work, because I am able to come up with many things that do make sense and tell the benefit of drinking an energy drink. All I do is follow a simple process of very basic questions and concise answers, until I find a "true" situation. Once there, I introduce the product (or not).

So, you now know one of the methods I use. Don't feel obliged to try it if it doesn't convince you. Whether you do or not, I am still convinced that any renowned creative person asks many questions to reach the conclusions that lead to their greatest ads. Therefore, I recommend that when you have a brief in front of you, you put yourself in the shoes of your most inquisitor self and ask loads of questions. That is the path that will give you the answer you are looking for.

~

Chapter 3

DON'T JUDGE IDEAS too QUICKLY.

> "If you want creative workers,
> give them enough time to play."
> **John Cleese**

Nothing frustrates and blocks your creativity more than your creative partner instantly shutting down any suggestion with negativity. A good idea sometimes might come from a bad one, a silly comment or a nonsensical thought. The best ideas often do. So take a ruler with you and do not hesitate to punish any castrating and negative co-workers with whom you have to work, day in day out. In my years as an advertising creative, I have reached an irrefutable conclusion. The partners who are the fastest to say "no" are undoubtedly the worst.

Let me tell you a little story. A few months ago, while teaching at Miami Ad School, I did a little experiment to check how the students were coming up with ideas. Do they come up with things randomly? Do they ask questions? Do they have a method? I wanted to know, so I used several students, put them into pairs to brainstorm and listened to them while they worked. I listened quietly for a minute, then left (feigning an urgent need for coffee or the bathroom) before returning a few minutes later to see how they had gone.

In most cases, I returned to absolute silence and blank poker faces. How could they be stuck after only 5 minutes? What did they do wrong? Well, pretty much everything.

First, they let their ego emerge and prevented their partner from expressing themselves freely. Sometimes a few criticising words were enough to destroy the idea; "I don't like it" or "I'm not sure". Often a sceptical look would break the wings of that poor idea moments after it had come out of the mouth of the other person.

Second, and probably even more destructive, was their negative attitude towards the brief that escalated at a frantic pace. "The brand is shit", "the product is rubbish", "this exercise does not make any sense", "can't we work on Wonderbra or Harley-Davidson instead?". They may not have come up with ideas, but their ability to come up with excuses was out of this world.

Above all, what hurt their chances of coming up with good ideas the most was how often they used the word "no". It came out of their mouths faster than a child demanding sweets in a candy shop. Even before their partners had finished telling the whole idea, he/she was often interrupted with a sentence along the lines of: "No, this brand would never do that."; "No, this idea is not good", "No, our target group is 3 years older". "No, no, no, etc…". And while I was observing them, I could not help but think how many interesting thought-starters they were judging and killing prematurely. How could they not realise that they were becoming the killers of their own creativity. In the end, all of them just looked at me and said, "Help Santiago, we're stuck."

They weren't aware of why they couldn't come up with ideas, and that's because they had not yet learnt an important lesson: in a brainstorming session, "no" should be avoided like the plague. "No" closes doors, roads and paths. "No" makes it impossible for new ideas to emerge. "No" gives you the self doubt to kill your next idea before it can escape your mouth.

In an ideal world, where creatives have left their ego outside the office door, brainstorming sessions should be treated as exercises of generosity, sharing and nurturing. Brainstorming is when we encourage one another's delicate little ideas, developing them instead of blowing them into oblivion.

The first stage of brainstorming should be used to think broadly and freely. Free to say what we want. Free to talk nonsense. Free to laugh at our own ideas. Free to start thinking about the wrong target audience.

This freedom creates the perfect environment to conduct a brainstorm: that type of environment where everyone can express themselves free from judgement. Why destroy other people's ideas before they have even formed and taken shape? Why not let that little embryo grow into something better? Who knows, maybe if we give it a chance, that idea might turn into a campaign to be remembered for several generations (alright, this is a little optimistic, but pardon me for being a dreamer).

So we understand each other a little better, I would like to share with you a story from my Argentine ex-colleague Fede about the need to create the perfect thinking environment. He began his career as a publicist in Buenos Aires, where talented people filled every corner of the local agencies. The start to his career was tough and he wasn't able to hold a position for too long. As he put it, "I was lucky to get an offer from my own mother, let alone (the agency) Mother Buenos Aires". He told me about his experience there and how they came up with ideas. Being, like many others, a big fan of that agency, I listened attentively to what he said.

What came out of his mouth seemed the most generous, positive and rewarding environment for brainstorms I had ever heard in my life. And not only did it sound great, but as one of the most iconic Latin agencies of the last decade, it was clearly productive too.

First of all, the briefs were not distributed hierarchically. There was no such thing as the "good brief" that only the two creative directors could work on, while everyone else worked on utter crap. Teams did not work on different clients either. No, when there was a need to come up with a campaign, the entire creative department gathered in a room to come up with ideas. Yes, altogether.

The brainstorming session was supervised by the agency's creative lead, who did not use his position of power to punish ideas, but to make sure that not a single idea died prematurely. To this effect, they established a rule that meant every idea had to be discussed for at least 30 minutes. Regardless of the quality of what had come out of that creative's mouth. If someone said "we could do a piece of shit stuck on a stick" they would discuss that said shit on a stick for half an hour and let it survive until it died on its own. If it ever died.

Fede told me that sometimes he felt embarrassed by peoples' ideas, but that didn't matter in the least. The whole team continued to let the thinking of each of its members flow, hoping that something would develop into the agency's next big idea. This is an unusual method, but it has to be one of the most enriching I have ever heard.

An agency sufficiently sure of itself to allow a free flow of ideas, free of early judgments and castrating attitudes (that no doubt have killed so many good thoughts over the years). Not everyone has the mentality, resource or the structure to do things like Mother Buenos Aires, but we should all consider their tolerant attitude.

If creatives weren't so prone to proving their worth by diminishing other people's ideas, if sometimes we accepted our partners and colleagues ideas as better than our own, then advertising would achieve utopian levels of excellence.

But, for now, I'm happy to ask you to let ideas live, to play with them like children would. To not kill thoughts no matter how dumb they sound. Give them a chance. Next time you brainstorm, play a little game and avoid saying "no" for half an hour or so. Listen to everything first before you judge. There's always time to get rid of ideas that aren't good enough later.

You know, I have had the chance to work with talented creatives and others that were not that talented but who were super methodical. There's no question that my best campaigns did come out with the methodical partners. With them, the ideas did not die after only a few seconds or minutes. We often came back to rubbish thoughts days and weeks later to polish them, and polish them again, until something stuck. Sometimes they were polished enough to become as shiny as a Bronze, Silver or Gold Lion.

Yes, you can also win those awards! You just need to say "no" a little less.

~

Chapter 4

EVERY IDEA has its MOMENT.

> "Nothing is more powerful than an idea whose time has come."
> **Victor Hugo**

There are two things in which I consider myself the champion of the galaxy: the first is buying things under 100 euros, the second is being in the right place at the right time – and somehow not taking advantage of it. Missing perfect Hollywood moments to declare my love to a girl has happened to me more times than I want to remember (you know the type, something extraordinary happens and that beautiful girl lands on your lap as if by magic). Not betting on a sport result while my instinct was screaming "Go ahead Santi, you're going to get rich" has happened to me even more. But no missed opportunity hurts more than having a great idea and doing nothing about it.

One random day, you get up from bed (or not) and have a brilliant idea. You imagine your boss' smile, feel the pat on your back, and picture a thick bundle of money falling from the sky directly into your pocket. But then your optimism deflates. In seconds, self doubt and pragmatism begin to eat away at you. You begin to think, maybe your idea is not that great, then you start worrying about how hard it would be to make, fighting against the world to carry it out. In an instant you've lost your energy.

But what you don't know is that just like you, another guy in Dubai or Djibouti has had the same idea. Only he or she is willing to fight for it. In fact, they're probably already in production. They've made the effort you have not. And a few months, weeks or even days later, you see your idea on Ads of the World or another advertising website. Of course you are quick to say, "I had that idea, I had that idea". But nobody believes you. Even if they do, no one cares. You will not be on the credits, nor at the stage in Cannes picking up a Lion for it. Tough luck!

There are hundreds of thousands of creatives trying to find imaginative solutions to similar problems for nearly identical clients. We observe the world under the same microscope with many of the same references. It's not surprising then that we often come up with similar solutions.

For example, in recent years, you will have noticed how many socially oriented campaigns have emerged in advertising. So many brands are trying to make us believe that they make the world a better place, that a can of soda can give women a voice or restore peace to the middle east, that a football brand can help find organ donors, that an automotive, beauty or food brand can save lives. We reach similar conclusions, because so often we are trying to achieve the same thing. That is why it is not surprising that in our industry you so often hear "it's been done to death" or "it's already done".

Advertising almost feels like a race sometimes. Here are a couple of examples of recent campaigns that I saw first in student portfolios many years ago. As student campaigns, they went completely unnoticed. A few years later, other creatives had the same ideas and produced them in agencies – and ended up winning more awards than you can wish for in an entire career. The campaigns are "Interception" by Volvo and "McWhopper" by Burger King.

Volvo.
As it happens every year, the US celebrates the famous Super Bowl that becomes the most watched annual sporting event on the planet. Brands spend tens of millions to have their ads broadcast during the game and car companies are undoubtedly the ones that invest the most. In 2015, Volvo was the smartest of them all. They managed to become the number one trending topic without spending a single cent. How did they do it? Simple. They came up with an idea called "Interception" (Image 03). The idea, which could have occurred to all of us in my opinion, was to giveaway a free top-of-

the-range Volvo during the match. So far it sounds like any number of boring promotions you've probably seen before. But what made it special is, to win, you had to tweet #Volvo during another car brand's multi million dollar commercial. At the end of the game, the statistics were overwhelming. Every time one of Volvo's competitors commercials ran, all the discussion on Twitter was about #Volvo instead. For the duration of the Super Bowl, it was the most talked about product in the world. While Mercedes, BMW and the rest spent more than 50 million on ads, Volvo spent nothing and was still the most mentioned car.

When I think of "Interception," I cannot help but remember the students who had the same idea in their portfolio (for another brand) and the many other creatives who have probably thought of it at some point. Proof that it's not enough to just think of good ideas. You have to make them too. Whether or not they were the first people to think of the idea, the creatives at Grey New York were the first to carry it out and simply speaking "they killed it".

Burger King.
One day in 2016, I woke up in the morning and opened my Linkedin. As soon as I looked at my wall, I discovered that that today is "Peace day": the official day for peace on Earth. I know this because all my contacts had just shared and commented on a campaign called "McWhopper".

EVERY IDEA HAS ITS MOMENT

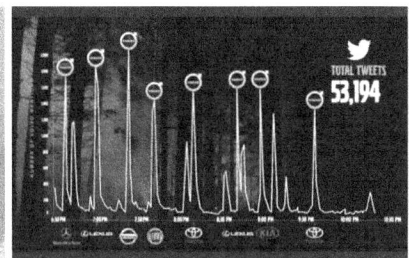

Image 03

Image 04

What was it about? Well, Burger King proposed to co-create a new hamburger with their biggest rival, McDonalds: the McWhopper (a perfect mix of the Big Mac and the Whopper) (Image 04). The idea was to symbolically put an end to their commercial rivalry and inspire the world to seek peace.

As a skeptical advertising creative, I find it impossible to believe that Burger King's intention was truly to promote any kind of peaceful feeling in the world. But it is also true that from a marketing point of view, Burger King took McDonalds by the balls and put them against wall. McDonalds didn't accept the offer of creating the McWhopper, claiming that war was way more serious a subject than a simple commercial rivalry. The CEO also added that next time Burger King wanted to collaborate "a simple phone call would do", as opposed to huge PR campaign and a print ad in a famous american newspaper. In the world of advertising, the truth is that, had McDonalds accepted the offer, it would have meant accepting that Burger King had been smarter and more opportunistic than them. So even the search for peace on earth was not enough to bring these two rivals together.

Peace Day was there for all brands to use. BMW could have proposed to Mercedes to release a "BMerc" on that very day. Kit-Kat and Twix could have created a "TwixKit" or Adidas and Nike could have done the same with some of their most iconic sneakers.

But again, it doesn't matter if you have an idea. It only matters if you make it come true. Then it becomes immortal. At least for the people working in the advertising industry. In this case, it was two guys from New Zealand who turned this idea into one of the most opportunistic ideas in history. Even more so if you consider that this famous hamburger, the "McWhopper" never saw the light of day. An idea that never came to be but reached eight billion impressions on the internet.

The road for the McWhopper was never easy though. The idea was first presented in New Zealand, but Burger King's CEO was against it. It went round in circles for a long time. The creatives didn't despair and they continued to fight for their idea over the next two years, until they managed to get it across to the Marketing Director of BK USA. When he heard it, he instantly loved it. The two Kiwis got their reward. They knew that their idea was worth it and they fought for it.

That same idea, the "McWhopper", had been languishing in a student's folio for a long time. But that's how far it went. It is easy to think now of the student biting his fingernails and repeating to everyone "I had that idea, I had that idea". But it doesn't matter and no one cares. I'm sure other people had that idea too. But in the award annuals, you'll only find the names of a couple of creative guys from New Zealand who gave the idea of the McWhopper its moment.

Apart from these masterful examples, there are two other campaigns that I would like to comment on, mainly because they touched me closely.

Close Unicef.

A few months ago I saw a poster on the street that caught my attention (Image 05). It did so for two reasons: one because it made me curious; the other, because finally a professional had made and idea that I had heard hundreds of times before. #CloseUnicef was the name of the idea and it came out of the hands of JWT Madrid.

However, I could not stop thinking about how many times I had heard the same idea. The first time was when I was still a student at Miami Ad School and three classmates (Virginia, Manu and Cris) had thought up a great idea that would lead them to be named students of the year in the D&AD contest. The idea was identical to #CloseUnicef but for Oxfam. The same thing. Exactly. The only difference was that Oxfam was a student idea created for an advertising festival. The other one a real campaign, which had been produced and released.

The curious thing is, that from the moment I heard those students talk about their #CloseOxfam campaign it took seven long years before someone could make it for real. Seven years in which I kept thinking "when will a professional make this campaign?". Why was I asking myself that question?

Simply because that idea seemed to follow me everywhere I went. For years I kept hearing the same exact sentence from loads of different people: "I have a great idea for an NGO. The idea is to shut the NGO down to catch people's attention." I heard that idea in Madrid, I heard it in Paris, I also heard it in Prague. If I worked in more agencies I'm sure I would have heard it even more.

Image 05

Either way, Unicef had the courage to do it, or maybe JWT knew how to sell the idea better than all the other agencies who thought of the same thing. Whatever happened, I'm sure the creatives at JWT celebrated its success. For me, above all it was a relief. I would not have to hear it anymore. Its time had finally come.

The First website you can eat.

A few years ago, I was lucky enough to work at a wonderful agency called Remo. One of those places in which as soon as you start, you are made to feel part of the family. I remember the nights out every Thursday, the hangovers on Fridays and the brunches we had as we finished our working week.

Anyway, one day I was working on a brief for Giovanni Rana, a huge Italian brand that sells fresh pasta but that thinks it's enough to do an ad every five or six years.

So, they wanted to come up with a promotional idea for people to try their products and their budget was about a ridiculously small 3000 euros. A little less than the price of the bicycle that decorates the lobby of their offices in Milan. For us though, making ideas with really low budgets had already become the norm, so it didn't stop us from being positive about finding something decent.

We got down to work and after a couple of days of brainstorming, my partner came up with a pretty fun idea. We were going to create "the first website you can eat": a microsite full of ravioli that you could taste virtually. By clicking on your ravioli of choice, you would get a voucher to redeem a pack of Giovanni Rana from the store.

Ok, it wasn't the idea of the century, but we were all happy to present it to the client, and even more so when the client gave us the go ahead. But no one could have predicted what was about to happen. Literally a week after we had finished producing the idea and were sharing it with the world, ING Direct celebrates their anniversary by releasing a website made of a huge cake that you can click on to eat. Plagiarism! Robbery! Motherf******! (Image 06).

Hearing the angry raised voices in our office, our creative director came instantly to see what happened. To our surprise, he almost did not react when he saw that a similar idea had come out at the same time as ours. According to him, these things happen in advertising. There are many people thinking about similar products and many come up with the same idea. Tough but true.

Image 06

The worst part is that although our idea had come out first, ING had spent a lot more money in making their edible website. As a result, theirs looked better and it was worth an award at the Spanish festival. Meanwhile, we were almost taken to the nearest hospital by an anxiety attack.

But this is not the end of the story. No. A few months later, once I had recovered from that trauma, I decided to leave Remo (Madrid) and take my backpack with me to find work in another European agency. As if it was the déjà vu of the déjà vu, each and every one of the creative directors I showed my portfolio to told me: "Oh, I had the same idea for such and such a client". I could not believe it. Our "first website you can eat", was only the first to have seen the light because of sheer luck. It could have as easily been the "the twenty-third website you can eat". Just another proof that every idea has its moment. Sometimes it depends on you, sometimes it doesn't.

~

Chapter 5

the answer is one millimeter away

Paul Gauguin

Tony Robbins, the coaching guru, said that one of his clients, a famous plastic surgeon, had determined the proportions of the perfect face. According to him, if the distance from the nose to the mouth was equal to the length of your eye, the person was considered beautiful. If the distance was one millimeter more or less, the person was considered normal. And if the distance was greater or shorter than two millimeters, that unfortunate person was to be considered ugly.

Although this story is just an anecdote, it is true that in life, we are often much closer to our goal than we first think. Sometimes the greatest idea is just a millimeter away from an idea we deem average. In fact, since we are talking about measurements, I'd like to share the best idea I have ever heard. It's not an advertising idea, but it is a huge marketing idea that started with something really really tiny.

A few years ago, the Colgate group brought together many of their worldwide marketing chiefs to find a way to increase their sales. At first, they gravitated towards the natural solution: a global campaign. They would invest millions in brand advertising and wait for the increased sales to slowly roll in. But during the brainstorming session, one of them had a much better idea; an idea that literally changed Colgate by half a millimeter but had huge implications on their profits.

It was as simple as altering the design for the tube of toothpaste itself. It occurred to one of the marketing chiefs that they could sell more toothpaste by simply making the hole where the toothpaste comes out half a millimeter bigger. People would still squeeze the toothpaste like normal, and soon without even noticing, they'd go back for more Colgate a little more often. The execs were spot on and that year their sales skyrocketed. All because they had made a hole half a millimeter larger.

In my career as a creative, I have failed on many occasions because I thought that good ideas could only come after a sustained period of effort; after you have complained about every single sentence in the brief, when you have gone through despair and anxiety, questioning your abilities and wallowing in self doubt for night after sleepless night. I thought, only then after so much mental tension could a worthy idea appear. God, how wrong I was!

On many occasions I suffered the misfortune of rejecting a simple idea that I deemed too obvious – only later to see the same one being presented by another colleague and approved by the Creative Director, then the client, then the production company and so on and so on.

It happened to me while working in Spain on the Insurance company, Acierto.com. I had spent weeks working on the brief with my former creative partner, trying to create something as creative as their previous campaigns. I wanted to come up with elaborated and smart stories. I presented all types of work: funny, emotional, serious… I tried them all out on friends, family, waiters and street vendors. Everyone laughed at our creativity and genius. But it didn't matter.

Another creative team from the agency had a much simpler idea. One that had crossed my mind in the first five minutes. We would see a man renewing his car insurance without checking prices on Acierto.com. Then the brand icon, a huge hand, would give the reckless insurer the thumbs down, smashing the guy into the floor as he went to buy his insurance with another company. While I first dismissed it as banal, obvious and not very creative, I continued for days trying to find the perfect idea. Meanwhile my partner (who is very much still my friend) decided to present it to the boss, and the boss to the client, and finally from the television to millions of customers.

The same thing happened to me again with Arsys.com. Arsys is similar to Wix, Squarespace, Cargocollective – allowing you to create a professional website easily. They wanted to launch a campaign to reaffirm their position as market leaders in Spain.

As soon as I started thinking of ideas, the first thing that came to my mind was to make a TV spot that showed the protagonist finishing his site on Arsys. The second he went out onto the street, suddenly everyone knew him and greeted him. My partner thought that the idea was too basic and I thought he was right. Not only was it basic, but it was the first idea that had come to mind, and that usually means it's crap. So we kept on thinking of all kinds of new ideas; weird, funny and absurd. But nothing felt great. So after a few days filling our office board with concepts and ideas, the Creative Director entered our office.

He asks us how we are doing and tells us that he has an idea that we can run with. "The idea was to make a TV spot whose protagonist had just finished creating his website on Arsys, and the minute he went out on the street, it turned out that everyone knew him and greeted him." Yes, he was telling us the same idea that we came up with almost a week ago after a few minutes of thinking. For him the idea was basic but it worked and responded perfectly to the brief. I was perplexed and even annoyed to see that the effort of several days of work was not going to be of any use and that he was going to use an idea that was mine, his, but mine!

Seeing my puzzled face, he asked me "what's wrong Santiago?" I answered that I had that same idea days ago. That it had taken us a few minutes of thinking to come up with it. He simply replied that "sometimes, those are the best ideas" and left the office. Now, I don't know if there's some truth in what he said, but I do know that 'his' idea was presented to the client a day later, shot a week after that and broadcast on YouTube by the end of the month.

So, my dear friends, if there's something I'd like you to gain from this chapter, it is the fact that sometimes, we tend to complicate things too much. We dismiss things for being too obvious, we believe that an idea is only valid if it has arisen after hours and hours of picking your brain until it bleeds and you've gone half mad. It's not. Humans are complicated beings, and creatives even more so. But as complicated as we are, we all prefer simple ideas. And the ones that reach everyone, tend to be.

Therefore do not reject your ideas only because they appeared too easily or too soon. Sometimes, ideas are much closer than we realise. Think as freely as a beginner and love all your ideas (that way there'll be no Creative Director making your idea "his").

Chapter 6

HAVE you EVER READ the BRIEF?

> "The shortest answer is doing the thing."
> **Ernest Hemingway**

There is no specific format for a brief but it should supposedly include some of the following information:

— The brand's name.
— The brand's background.
— The product you're advertising.
— The consumer to whom the campaign is directed (often called the target audience).
— Market trends or particular relevant insights about the product or audience.
— The objectives of the campaign.
— The delivery date and deadlines for the campaign.

For creatives, that's often all the information you will receive. No one will bother telling you the production budget for that campaign. Best assume the answer is "as cheap as possible".

Usually the client provides a brief that is first edited and prepared to make a little more sense by the account or planning teams. Then a briefing is held in the agency and the account people share with the creatives the objectives and mandatories of the campaign. At this point, there are two types of creatives: those who listen carefully and ask more or less relevant questions about the brief, and those who wait for the meeting to finish to go back to their desk and break the brief into a thousand pieces before throwing them all in the bin.

I must admit, I have been both types of creative. Both the one who asks questions and the 'brief destroyer'. The truth is, I was always better off when I used the brief than when I didn't. Not because it necessarily led to better ideas, but because I managed to get them more easily and with much less effort.

So I invite you to rethink your initial disregard for the briefs you're handed. Next time, try the following: forget the voice in your head that tells you the account department is no help. Instead give them some extra work. When you get a brief, ask them to write as much info as possible, tell your account colleagues not to condense anything. Tell them that you'd rather do that yourself. In the process of writing as much as possible, they will expand their thoughts, perhaps uncovering new thought starters or even particular words or descriptions that prove to be a helpful springboard into an idea.

If the people working in accounts have even an iota of interest in their job (which is usually the case), they will write everything you need to know in order to find interesting ideas. Their own writing and personal way of explaining things will be full of clues, words and sentences that can trigger an idea.

That's how I got my ideas for a pitch, a pitch I had absolutely no interest in and from which all other creatives fled as if it were the plague. The pitch I am talking about was for a tobacco brand which I have tried desperately hard to permanently scrub from my memory.

The brief for the tobacco brand which name I do not want to remember went along the lines of the following:

"The mix of experiences makes life richer. That is why our tobacco brand believes that a good cigarette is the result of the richness and diversity in its mixture: combining the softness of Virginia tobacco with the richness of a dark Burley and the velvety Oriental softness. This makes our cigarettes full of character. Therefore, as we are convinced that rich experiences are only the result of contrasted mixtures, we have committed ourselves to encourage mixtures of ideas and experiences since 1896. To promote aromatic life experiences (yes they really do write such bollocks) *that are nothing less than magnificent chaos, in which the pleasure comes from finding people with depth and emotions. Knights*

of style, dancers, physicists and strollers of the tightrope, all in conversation together. In which music is always heard and refined at the same time, just so you can let your feelings blossom. Yes, we believe that true wealth is created through beautiful mixtures, not just beautiful things. So if you are like us, and believe that richness is a matter of blending, come and join us."

On top of this drivel, they added that the campaign should of course respect the style and laws governing cigarette ads. Which simply means, according to the high and low statutes defined by the advertising quality control bodies, all you can really say is nothing whatsoever. You cannot say "smoke our cigarettes because they taste good", "smoke because you'll look cooler" or "smoke because it's amazing".

The only appropriate message for a tobacco ad is none at all; tobacco advertising is reduced to finding a silly trick that includes the color of the brand, the taste, or how the tobacco is made. In some cases, you have to invent some higher philosophy of life that sounds like something new but in reality has been said innumerable times before.

Basically you must create a message to sell tobacco without saying anything that encourages the purchase of tobacco. Incredible but true. It's like saying to your son "run to the store but at the same speed as if you were walking".

Now if that poor analogy doesn't help you understand cigarette advertising, perfect, because this state of semi-confusion is exactly what every creative forced into a tobacco brief is reduced to.

But let's go back to the brief, and to my process: without hesitation after reading that stuffy and boring paragraph full of fluff and millennial brand wank, I refused to think about ideas and instead decided to save my energy. Instead, I sat down, picked up a marker and began to highlight words that had some sparkle.

So I kept the following words:
Experiences, life, rich, blend, velvety (velvet).

Right after, I simply started making combinations based on those words. This was the result:

Experience the rich life.
Blend with life.
Blend with the rich life.
Life is a matter of blend.
Blend with the velvet life.
Life is velvet.
Experience the velvet life.
"Live the velvet life!"
Bingo!

I had just picked up the brief, chose some words and put them together. Now, with just a few combinations doodled on a piece of paper, here was a solution that worked perfectly and that I had no doubts could be presented to the boss of the 'tobacco brand which name I do not want to remember': "Live the velvet life".

While we had reduced coming up with the idea to a child's game, the next task would be harder; creating hundreds of visuals and posters to incorporate "Live the velvet life" as a tagline. My copywriting job lasted 15 minutes. My Art Director's would last the following five days.

~

WALLS

Chapter 7

ARE UNINSPIRING.

> "To acquire knowledge, one must study;
> but to acquire wisdom, one must observe."
> **Marilyn vos Savant**

When I started studying advertising, I remember attending a class called Ad Concepts. Our teacher was Paco Conde, now an international advertising star, at the time a well-known Creative Director in Madrid. I absolutely loved his classes because you could see how interested he was in making you learn. I also remember how embarrassed I was to show my ideas to him and how comforting his feedback was. But what I remember the most is something he said that had little to do with my concepts, and a lot to do with the birth of ideas.

> "Get out of school. Do not stay locked inside here.
> The answers are out there."

Now that made sense at the time, but it wouldn't be until a few years later that I put this advice into practice. I was in desperate need of ideas on a pitch for the household appliance brand Balay, and after several days of thinking inside the office, I could not pick one thought that had any potential.

That day, Paco Conde came to my mind and I remembered how he commented the importance of observing people's behavior to find ideas (as it so happens, John Hegarty regularly preaches the same advice). Since I had nothing to lose, I went to the place I thought was easiest to find loads of people doing random things: Atocha, the main railway station in Madrid.

I asked for a decaf coffee with milk and no sugar, as I always do. I turned off my phone, took out my pencil and notebook. There I was sitting on my own, surrounded by thousands of people, wondering exactly how I had ended up there on a Sunday afternoon.

I began watching these strangers, hoping to find inspiration for a washing machine commercial, as they talked to their friends and families. I was sceptical, of course, doubting my choice in relevant location; no one in the railway station was going to show up with a washing machine, let alone buy one.

However, I soon saw the benefits. Observing people was like opening a book full of insights. It did not matter whether or not they were buying washing machines or using them. In advertising, the brand matters less than the consumer and there in Atocha, I was surrounded by hundreds of consumers as they went about their lives.

Unknowingly, they were giving me all sorts of clues about

human behaviour: I could observe how they rushed to get out of the trains, last minute shopping, impatient waiting for their loved ones. And would you believe it, but each one of these moments led me to an equivalence within the glamorous world of washing machines with a built-in tumble dry function. In my mind, the rush to leave the station became the rush to have clothes washed and dried. Last minute purchases became the last minute washing before a trip – the situation when a washing machine with drying function would be ideal. In my head, waiting impatiently for a loved one became a scene where you're desperately waiting for your clothes to dry on a humid day. The perfect moment for a Balay. In a matter of minutes, I had more answers written in my notebook than in two days looking at the ceiling of my office.

No, ladies and gentlemen. Looking at the walls of an agency is not inspiring. We always raise our heads when we think. It is human nature. But looking at a ceiling doesn't help. You could look at a candle flame for three days and get the same number of ideas: one if you're lucky and zero in all probability.

That's why Miguel Vizcaíno (Paco Conde's ex-boss), the founder of the agency Sra. Rushmore and one of the best-known Spanish creatives outside our borders, did not stay in the office to think about ideas either. When working on a campaign for a banana brand, he decided to go to all the grocery stores and spend hours watching how people bought bananas, because in the course of those purchases, someone would do something peculiar enough that it could become a creative idea that the rest of consumers would empathize with. If he did not find the answer in a store, he would go to another until something struck him.

But going to stations, shops or parks isn't the only thing you can do to increase your chances of being inspired. Everyone needs to find their own method. Train stations work for me. Maybe watching a movie works best for you. Films are full of human insights, stereotypes and truths that we often plague advertising commercials with. Go to the cinema on your own for once. Concentrate on watching the movie not as a spectator but as an investigator. I guarantee that if you do that correctly, you will also get ideas.

Some will say, okay, I'm going to see how people buy bananas: easy. But what if I have to make an ad for Harley-Davidson or Mercedes? Are you going to let me drive a motorcycle or go to the dealership to watch the buyers with a magnifying glass? Obviously not. Using the product or seeing how someone uses it can help you get ideas, but observing people in general is so powerful that it doesn't always matter if they are interacting with that product or not. People, wherever they are, are an inexhaustible source of consumer behaviors. Observing them will always increase your chances to get inspired.

My point is: leave the office for a moment. Go for a walk. Look at people and write down what you see, what they do. Look for equivalences with the brand you are desperately trying to find ideas for, and if you open your eyes and mind a little, thoughts will flow.

An office ceiling is flat, limiting and uninspiring. The world out there has a lot more life and colour. So, do not wait for your ideas to appear! Go find them.

"The answers are out there".

~

Chapter 8

If you LIKE it, TAKE it.

Pablo Picasso

The world of advertising has changed a lot in recent years and it will continue to do so until the end of time. However, one thing will always remain the same: the way we as advertising creatives are inspired.

If an idea crosses our mind, its origin is undoubtedly a result of the different things we have seen, experienced, read and heard in our life. It is hard to be a great creative without having a curious personality. But these days, with social networks and our unlimited connectivity, we are fed hundreds of different things on a daily basis. Whether we are curious or not, we are inundated with inspiration.

An ongoing question for creatives is; can we use or reference something we've seen on the internet for our campaigns?

There are many opinions on this subject. I myself was strongly against anyone who appropriated a music video, film, technique or artwork and recreated it blatantly for the brand.

Many creatives feel the same way about appropriation. But over time, my opinion has changed radically. Why? Because I was fortunate enough to work with the lifelong creative inspiration, Gerardo Silva. He changed the way I saw things with one simple question.

One pleasant sunny day, working in Madrid, I was looking at an advertising blog when I came across a Lego campaign that recreated cartoon characters. A German agency had released the campaign and suddenly it was all over social networks, widely receiving praise. My response was far less positive. I was outraged. This campaign was based on the work of a student who had posted the original on Behance, and now some agency had lifted his idea. I started ranting against the advertising industry, internet thieves and even the noisy office chinchilla.

My partner Gerardo, saw how agitated I was and asked the reason for my anger. When I explained to him the greatest robbery in the history of advertising, he looked at me and said: "Santi, why do you think advertising agencies are full of old photography books?"

IF YOU LIKE IT, TAKE IT

norwegian.com

Brad is single
Los Angeles. From/one way, incl taxes.

£169*

*Start your journey from London-Gatwick (LGW). Travel between 20 January 2017 – Feb 2017. Book by 26th September 2016. The fare is based on our lowest one way direct economy fare incl. taxes and charges excl. weekends, school and public holidays. Restrictions and baggage fees may apply. Fare correct as of 20 September 2016.

Image 07

Image 08

Image 09

I didn't understand. What did photography books have to do with stealing the work of a student? Gerardo looked at me and explained, what I had just discovered was in fact something that had happened since the beginning of times in advertising. And for that matter, there was nothing wrong with it.

What creatives are doing now with inspiration lifted from the internet is no different from what creatives did two decades ago with photography books. If they came across something worthwhile, they just copied the technique or the style and used it for their campaign. Of course, no one bothered to call the photographer and ask if he was ok with the agency doing something 'similar'.

What lesson should we draw from all this? Well, as I said in the previous chapter, when you have a brief in your hands, you should keep an eye on what is happening around you and not be afraid to take it. The world of advertising is full of personalities with egos larger than an Olympic stadium. You must be ruthless (although many will deny it) and you must pay attention to everything that happens in the world.

Take advantage of the breakup of one of the most famous couples in Hollywood, Angelina Jolie and Brad Pitt, to make an ad as fun and simple as the one made by the staff at Norwegian airlines (Image 07). A print ad that nearly every agency in the world could have run it for one their brands. Far from looking like an obsolete media, campaigns like this have given print advertising a second life.

Take advantage of Donald Trump's election in order to make a joke like "Trumpdonald.org" (Image 08) created by the Swedish agency Animal. A wonderful and addictive platform in which the only purpose is to ruffle the controversial politician with trumpet sounds and confetti while he follows you with his eyes. A very unique way to self-promote your agency and drive people to your website.

Take advantage of Scotland's referendum, just like a French duo did as soon as it was announced that Scotland voted to remain in Britain. They made an ad for Scotch tape, recreating the Scottish flag by making a cross with sellotape and adding copy that read, "Scotch. We keep things together".

Kit-Kat also took advantage of another referendum (Brexit) to make slightly different packaging for their products. For a long time, the brand's purpose has been to champion the break. So, when the English voted "no" to staying in Europe, the famous chocolate changed the colors of its packaging and transformed them into a separated European and British flag accompanied by their famous "Take a Break" (Image 09). Having a concept line like "Take a break" made it easier for Kit-Kat to do something about a political break-up. But it would have been meaningless if it wasn't because the creative team were paying attention to what was happening in the world.

How about the blackout during the Super Bowl? Oreo created a simple ad that said "You can still dunk in the dark". The easiest ad ever. But a very opportunistic way of making the brand trending topic on one of the most important dates of the year.

I also remember how the acclaimed and retired creative Alex Bogusky tweeted that some insurance company should take advantage of the injury of a well-known American skier one day before the Olympics and make an ad with her. The guy had been retired for a while but was still paying attention and seeing opportunities better than anyone else. The next day, Liberty Insurance hired Heidi Kloser to be the image of their new campaign. A masterful way to take advantage of an event and a total freebie for the creative team (thanks Alex).

And who doesn't remember the highly addictive viral video of the weird stoned American discovering a double rainbow in Yosemite, California? In the face of such an event, the man went absolutely bananas and cried as if witnessing something divine. His "double rainbow" screams became a viral hit on YouTube. They even turned them into a musical success on iTunes. Soon enough, "Double Rainbow" became the idea for a Vodafone ad promoting double contracts.

That's just a few. We could go on and on with millions of other examples!

Put that through your mind: your next campaign is out there and everything that is out there is yours. Do not be afraid to take advantage of it. You just have to be the first to do it. Pay more attention to the world than you do when you are withdrawing your savings from an ATM at night in the dark alley of the scariest suburb.

Take advantage of any little opportunity you see. Ideas belong to everyone. The first one to grab the idea is often the one who grabs the Lion. Just so you know.

~

Chapter 9

ACCEPT your BRAND.

> "It's better to be absolutely ridiculous than absolutely boring."
>
> **Marilyn Monroe**

Over the years, brands have relied heavily on research and data to influence their communication strategy. While I appreciate the value of understanding what your consumer wants, I feel that the advertising industry can get carried away with data, random and poor research and wishful predictions.

In general, brands are so caught up in their soulless scientific studies that they forget what really matters: to communicate to their consumers who they are, why they exist and above all what makes them unique. They would prefer to be absolutely average, to use research to blunt any difference they started with, using committees and research groups to find the lowest common denominator idea and say the same thing we have heard a million times before. They are too afraid to take any sort of risk, find an original truth and give themselves a chance to stand out.

Thank god there are some brands and agencies who are brave enough to fight against convention, regardless of what marketing research may say. They come up with ideas that shook the world while still being honest and insightful.

Some of the agencies, creatives and marketing people I would like to thank from the bottom of my little heart are those who have produced campaigns for Marmite, Blokie and Hans-Brinker Hotel. As a result of their unusual communication, these brands have become some of my all-time favorites, even though the products themselves might look and feel like garbage. So, let's analyze what they do and how they do it.

Marmite.

Image 10

For those who are unfamiliar with it, Marmite is a sticky, extremely salty paste that is also edible (yes! I swear). It is manufactured and consumed mostly in the United Kingdom. Marmite's problem (or virtue) is that it has a very peculiar and powerful flavor. It is so unique that you either want to eat it like there's no tomorrow, or vomit.

In my case, the only time I ever tried Marmite, my displeasure was such that I assumed it was spoilt. It wasn't. That's genuinely how it's meant to taste. But funnily enough, the marketing and advertising cast this as a creative opportunity.

The advertising agency working on Marmite realized that this sticky paste had as many fans as it had haters so, instead of proposing a conciliatory message to convince the haters that Marmite was great for them, they simply told the truth: "You either love it or hate it" (Image 10).

To visualize these concept, their ads have gone as far as showing a jar of Marmite locked in the closet for years without being touched. They have shown mothers breastfeeding their children after eating Marmite, causing their baby to vomit. Their packaging even has a label that reads the word "I hate" under the logo.

More than just an example of bravery, this genius idea has caused precisely what every brand wants: for people to feel curious enough about their product to give it a try. Even if it's only once. Anyone that comes across a message from Marmite will automatically feel the need to know how Marmite tastes like. Trust me, I learnt that the hard way.

Yorkie.

This brand is perhaps a little less famous than Marmite, but they also show bravery in their communication. According to Marketing experts, Yorkie, was unsellable to men because men do not like chocolate (that makes me a woman then). I swear to God, this is what their research indicated. But, thank God, creativity was there to turn this problem into an opportunity (image 11).

The agency made a daring proposal: to release a new packaging with the unmistakably masculine name, Blokie. But the really bold move was to add a sentence under the logo that read, "Definitely a chocolate not suitable for women". To add insult, the letter "O" from Blokie was a symbol of a woman with a cross through it. With such an unusual relaunch, consumers were far too curious to not give the new Blokie chocolate bar a try. What was even more surprising (or not) is that the campaign boosted consumption amongst women. Yes, the very audience that wasn't targeted by Yorkie. More than ever, this campaign showed that women feel a fatal attraction for the things they cannot have, and that marketing research is not to be trusted.

Image 11

Hans-Brinker Hotel.

This is perhaps the most daring idea of all; one of the most powerful that every creative would like to have in their folio. For those who do not know Hans-Brinker, it is a cheap hotel located near the Red-Light district in Amsterdam. There's nothing special about it. Or maybe there is. In their ads, they claim to be "the worst hotel in the world". Yes, you have read that correctly. A brand is paying an agency to make an ad so that everyone knows that they are the worst on the planet.

The first ad I saw was titled "Accidentally eco-friendly" and is just one of their many examples of absurd honesty. In a grotesque tour of the hotel, the TV spot makes you discover an apocalypse of bad service: a hotel without the presence of a receptionist to greet you because he is too hungover and has

Image 12

fallen asleep at his desk. A hotel without hot water, toilet paper or soap bars. No windows. No working elevator, nothing. Simply, the worst hotel in the world (image 12). The hotel is so bad and the ad is so good that, again, I cannot help but be curious. I have promised myself that I would stay there next time I go to Amsterdam. Whatever the cost! My desire to pay for a bad experience is the proof that communication and creativity can change people's behavior in ways otherwise unimaginable. This idea should have been handed several Grand Prix in Cannes (sadly I don't believe it did).

Make no mistake, there are very few ads like these ones. Definitely not enough. I cannot help thinking that in part, agencies and creatives (myself included) are to blame. We are so used to embellish boring messages, and create the same sounding lines that we end up repeating ourselves. We forget the basics of our work: to find what makes a product special. As an ex-colleague once said, "the answer is in the product."

So, let's recharge our creative batteries. Let's spend more time looking at the product, playing with it, testing it, observing who consumes it, smelling it, hating it. Whatever is necessary to determine what makes it unique. There's always something! Always! When we have discovered what it is, let's try to turn it into an idea as great and unique as the product. Sometimes selling garbage is easier than selling gold.

Chapter 10

Get Recog- -nized.

> "You're not famous until my mother has heard of you."
> **Jay Leno**

Getting recognized is pretty difficult. For people and for brands. As humans, we dress like our peers' dress, we talk the way people around us talk, we cherish the same things our favorite classmates cherish. In other words, we might all wish to believe that we're totally unique, but in reality, we love the security of going along with the crowd. That non-adventurous feeling is so ingrained in us that, as creatives working in advertising, we are more likely to be comfortable with an idea that is 'already done' than one we've never seen before.

Generally speaking, 99% of brand communication strategies are the same as their competitors. They make the same type of products and they sell them using identical jargon and lines. A few examples come to mind:

In 1998, a year when Pepsi was claiming to be "The Joy of life", Coca-Cola could not come up with anything better than "Enjoy".

When Nike started using "Just do it", Asics, in a failed attempt to become people's sneakers of choice, ran with "Don't do it. Do it better". If it was in my hands, I would have fired the strategist and the copywriter who wrote that. Adidas also joined the party a few years later when they re-launched the brand with "Impossible is nothing". No matter how you look at it, it's a second-rate version of "Just do it" without the originality or charm. Nothing that comes second will ever be as cool as number one. Sorry Adidas.

And what about chocolate bars? While Kit-Kat has championed the break for years with the very popular "Take a break" tagline, Twix could not think of anything more original than "Pause".

How can we call ourselves creatives? We should call ourselves the copy and paste kings! The "recreatives". I thought the point of advertising was to communicate in a creative way by doing something different.

So why do we insist on copying our direct competitors? I have long thought about this, and the only answer I could come up with is that simply, we claim to have a winning mentality but we don't possess one. Our briefs are filled up with words such as "Change", "Different", "Innovative", "Fresh", "New" but then the ideas that get produced are the complete opposite.

When it's decision time we'd too often rather go safe, and think, "if our competitors are doing this, that's what we should be doing too." However, doing the opposite should be the answer. If this is what my competitor is doing, then I must do something radically different. Only then can I truly stand out.

So, let's take a moment to think about how certain brands have managed to become recognizable.

Sometimes the product possesses something recognizable or iconic. Take Guinness, for instance: their beer is darker and heavier with a lighter white froth. It looks different and it takes longer to pour. Two differences that have led to dozens of successful campaigns.

Sometimes the shape of the product is what makes it distinctive. Lego is a clear example. If you see a Lego piece, you just know it's Lego. There's nothing else like it (with the exception of Duplo, which is owned by Lego).

Sometimes the logo is so simple that it remains iconic decades after creation. The best example has to be Coca-Cola. After so many years, it remains unique, elegant and highly recognizable. Whether you see the font or the white wave, you know you're looking at a Coke. But Pepsi, after many redesigns over the years, could you think of their current logo? I'm not even sure what it looks like anymore.

These are very specific examples and the products mentioned are clearly distinguished from their competitors. Most brands don't have anything as unique, so as creatives, it is our task to search for something, perhaps in their history, or the way they're manufactured, or how they make consumers feel, or how they're consumed. If we don't find the distinctive story, instead we make one up. Whether it is a concept, a sound, a story, or a visual. We must create something unique to get seen. And when it is done well it is truly wonderful.

My favorite example of how a brand has managed to be recognizable for good reasons, and for its creativity is undoubtedly "Familiprix". You probably haven't even heard of them as they are a chain of Canadian pharmacies. The only reason I know them myself is because I collect the winning campaigns from each year's Cannes Lions. 50Gb of awarded pieces since 2002.

But back to Familiprix. Every ad starts with everyday life scenes. A lady cutting carrots at home, a woman shopping in a store, a man playing ice-hockey, etc. In all these scenes, we see the figure of a pharmacist standing and looking at these people as if he was invisible to them. Then all of a sudden, the people hurt themselves, bad. I mean it. The lady smashes her face against the shop door, the ice-hockey player breaks the glass of the ice rink, the lady cuts her fingers. As soon as they harm themselves, the pharmacist points to the victim with both arms raised and looks at the camera to shout, "Familiprix". A simple way of saying, if you get hurt, we have everything you need at our pharmacies.

It's a very simple series of ads, but the more examples you watch, the more you want to see. The greatness of these ads is that you feel you could come up with 100 new executions in one afternoon. The other admirable thing about the campaign is that it becomes like a game for the viewer. Once you recognize the figure of the pharmacist, you know it's a Familiprix ad, and that someone is going to get hurt. So, you try to guess who and how.

Familiprix have made simplicity and their tone the weapon that makes them recognizable. In a world where pharmacies never do anything wild, Familiprix decided to be an ironic brand. I suggest that you check it on YouTube and see it for yourself. For me that such a great campaign only won a Silver in Cannes leaves me skeptical about the legitimacy of award shows (but I could write a whole other book about that).

Anyways, let your mind play folks. Forget about what your competitors are doing. Or explore the exact opposite. Don't look to Ads of the World for your inspiration. With a bit of hard work and patience, you might actually come up with something that will not look like anything that has been done before.

Chapter 41

USE THE NAME of YOUR BRAND.

Zsa Zsa Gabor

There are hundreds of thousands of brands populating our planet and each year they spend a fortune creating more and more ads. The sheer number of ads we see each day (5,000 by some counts) makes it next to impossible for us to remember anything at all about any of them. And most campaigns fail even the most basic job of any ad: to have the audience remember the name of the brand.

But there is a way to avoid people forgetting the name of your brand. In fact, it's very simple. The more often a name is repeated, the more chances that it will stick in people's minds. So why not use it as your creative idea? After all, what client is not going to like the sound of their own name?

As simple and obvious as this may be, when it's time to create a campaign idea or tagline, creatives think in each and every direction, playing with words and ideas, but rarely starting with the brand's name. But why be so reluctant when it guarantees the impossible; the client will buy your idea.

To illustrate this, I would like to share with you several campaigns. They might not all go down in history as the greatest pieces of creative advertising, but they excel at something a lot of awarded campaigns often do not; they made their brands recognizable and memorable.

These campaigns were made by two creatives from Spain that I was lucky enough to work with for a few years and who are the inspiration behind this chapter: José Luis Moro and Pablo Torreblanca. Both made the inclusion of the brand's name in their work their trademark, and this trick has led them to make national campaigns for Spain's largest companies.

11811.

Image 13

Anyone who came across a brief for this client (an information service) would never think that you can do something creative with the name of a brand called '11811'. They would just try to find a funny or emotional idea and add '11811' at the end frame of the TV spot. But not José Luis Moro and Pablo Torreblanca. Here's the script they wrote (Image 13):

A one-year-old baby sits in a chair at a table with a plate of something that looks like pasta with a lot of tomato sauce on top of it. The baby is happily chewing that food, while the tomato fills his face, his bib, his arms and the rest of his body.

A number "1" sign appears on the screen while the voice-over says:

"One baby".

Again, another number "1" appears on the screen as the voice-over says: "One short-sighted nanny".

Another number "1" is added at the bottom of the screen and the voice-over continues: "One bottle of something that looks like tomato sauce".

Now number "8" appears on the screen, while we see the baby gesturing and making funny faces because of the food's taste. The voice-over says: "Eight tablespoons of tabasco".

Finally, another number "1" appears at the bottom of the screen, completing "11811". The voice over says: "One stupid video for you to remember a number that can be used for everything: from finding the number of a sports center to discovering the name of your favorite song. 11811. Get all the answers with a simple call."

This is a very simple and very effective too. Who could see this on TV and not remember which brand it was for? Furthermore, what client could hear an idea like this and reject it? Here's another example by the same creatives for the car company Ssangyong. A brand I did not even know until I saw this brilliant commercial.

Ssangyong.

Image 14

When you hear and see the spelling of Ssangyong, you can't help but think that it is virtually impossible to do something with that name, but José Luis Moro and Pablo Torreblanca pulled out another piece of magic and created a very fun ad that got them a few national awards (Image 14).

We open the ad with a still image of Beethoven, the famous musician. Over the image, the name Beethoven is misspelt. Throughout the ad, the text keeps changing but the name Beethoven is still not written correctly. These are some of the combinations we see: "Bethoveen", "Betoven", "Bhetoven", etc...

As we see that, the voiceover says: "Getting home and playing some Beethoven music in the background. Beethoven. How do you write that? Like this, or like that? Or this way? There's a 'h' somewhere, but I am not sure where it goes. What a strange name Beethoven! Bach is way easier. What happens with Beethoven is the same thing that happens with Ssangyong. No one really knows how to write it."

As with the word "Beethoven", we see a series of very diverse spellings for Ssangyong (San John, Sanyyunn, etc). All of them being misspelt.

The voice-over goes on: "But who cares? When you're cool, no one needs to know how to write your name. Isn't that right Beethoven?"

We close the ad, with a Ssangyong logo.

Well, I don't know your opinion but to me that is a masterful example of how in a simple way, with a good idea and using the name of the brand, you can create a good ad that customers will love and remember.

There are a lot of examples of course, but there's no need to see more of them, I think you get the point. So, next time you need to come up with an idea, and face a blank page do not look at the ceiling. From now on, always start by trying to do something with the name of the brand. If you manage, your client will buy the idea. I give you my word.

~

Chapter 12

THE POWER of SAYING yes.

> "When you say 'yes', the universe helps you."
> **Dan Brule**

Generally speaking, what Marketing Directors like to hear from their agencies are positive and cheerful ideas that they can pass on to the subconscious mind of the consumer. They love messages such as "buy me and you'll be happy." Nothing wrong with that. Everyone loves good vibes, positive things, and happiness. So, if a product transmits such values, a Marketing Director will feel that there will be more chances of a person buying into their message and the product.

Therefore, if we know that we should have positive ideas, our task as creatives is to find positive messages. I, fortunately, did not have to make great efforts to discover a key word that would save me on countless occasions. I discovered the power of the word "yes". I could use it in the taglines of many campaigns and it would save my ass. In case of a creative blockage, I just had to create a message with the word "yes" and I would be good to go.

Why? Because "yes" is the most positive word you can say. While "no" builds walls, "yes" demolishes them. "No" is limiting, "yes" gives you opportunities.

How did I discover the power of saying yes? A few years ago, when I worked in the agency Remo, in Madrid. At the time, Siemens, the famous household appliance brand was changing their creative strategy and was looking for a new agency to work with. Several high-level agencies were fighting to get that succulent piece of business capable of keeping afloat a small to medium sized agency, like the one I had the pleasure of working at.

All the creatives were working hard, aware of the importance of this pitch, knowing that a good concept would lead us to glory. The days passed by and the team's frustration grew as no one had an idea powerful enough to present to the client. Finally, after days of struggle to find an answer to the brief, a colleague came up with a tremendously simple idea. A brilliant message/tagline that made us confident that we would win the Siemens account.

The idea or concept was the following:

> "Siemens. The appliance brand that starts with 'Yes'.
> Please bear in mind that "Si" means "Yes" in Spanish.
> Si-emens = Yes-emens.

That was it. It may seem very simple and obvious, and it is. Of course, no one is going to win an international award or even a local one with that line, but I can assure you that this message is sweeter than a Chopin sonata to the ears of a person who works in marketing. It's like giving them a free ride to a world where their brand is the creator of happiness without the need of having to prove it.

It's simple. Way too simple to be true, but this trick can be repeated for any brand, even if its name does not start with "Si" ("Yes") as Siemens does.

But before getting into how this works with other brands, let's see the script that made us win the pitch and why 10 years later, the same idea has been rescued and shown again on television.

"Yes. Yes, it helps you. Yes, it pampers you. Yes, it suits you. Yes, it takes care of you. Yes. Yes, it lasts. Yes, it goes ahead. Yes, it surprises you. Yes, it saves time. Yes, it saves energy. Yes. Yes, it saves water. Yes, it loves you. Yes, you want it. Yes, it thinks of everyone. Yes, it thinks of you. Yes, it has everything you asked for in a household appliance. And yes, it consumes less energy and water."

"Siemens. The appliance brand that starts with "Yes".

Now "Siemens" might start with "sí", but the success of the campaign wasn't down to clever wordplay.

A few years later when I was working in Prague for Y&R, an international agency. As they sometimes did, the group Y&R sent us to different locations to help us solve briefs for big clients. This time, they had gathered a few creatives from Budapest, London and Prague in the offices of Barcelona to create a new campaign for Danonino. A Danone brand that clearly did not know how to tackle their communication strategy.

At first glance, the task we were given wasn't an easy one. A yoghurt brand that wanted to talk and promote the autonomy of children aged 3 to 5 via a custard-like milk product.

"What the hell?" I thought, and probably everyone else. After getting the brief and going for lunch together, every one of us retreated into our own corners and thoughts of ideas.

As it often happened to me at the time, I was not able to get ideas quickly. So, it was no surprise that the next day in the afternoon, when we had to do the first round of presentations, I was the only creative who had nothing decent to share. I have always hated these situations, because you are made to feel like you are less worthy than others. That your ideas define your personal value. So, after going through the shame of seeing how my ideas were discarded one by one, I began to review the tricks I had learned in my short creative life.

In a moment of relaxation, I remembered the Siemens campaign and how clients loved positive messages. I was sitting on a terrace under the agency, scribbling in my notebook when at some point, along with my colleague Psembi Kinstan, we came up with a sentence that would mark the beginning of a campaign: "Great stories start with YES".

It was infinitely worse than the Siemens tagline, but it was a good start. So, we continued giving it shape to present to the agency and see if it would make it to the client. In my mind, I had no doubt that the idea had potential, and if given a chance the Marketing team from Danone would buy into it. That's exactly what happened. A few days later, we officially presented four ideas to the client. Among them was "Great stories start with YES".

When we finished the meeting and it was time to go back to Prague, I was convinced that of all the ideas that had been discussed at that meeting, "Great stories start with YES" would be the one they would produce. Not because it was the best, but because it was the most positive. In fact, I think two other ideas were considerably better, but that did not matter one bit. Ideas don't win because they are creatively best, but because they are what best suits the client's vision.

A year later, time proved me right and the campaign I had created for Danonino with my colleague was on TV. The script had changed a little for the worse. The line too. But the word "Yes" was still the protagonist. Here it is:

A girl aged 4 appears in her room. She opens the closet and while looking at the camera, she says: "Mommy, can I get dressed alone?"

Cut and we see a child of the same age who looks at the camera and says: "Will you let me go to Dani's house?"

Cut again and we see another girl climbing some stairs leading to a tree house. While staring at the camera she goes. "Can I go play in the house?"

Cut and we see a series of images of children doing things by themselves, while some jolly music plays in the background.

Several sentences appear on screen:

"Sometimes, it's not easy to say yes... But what happens when we say it? We say yes to their confidence, yes to their autonomy, and yes to growing happy."

Finally, a girl starts dancing, while the Danonino logo appears on screen. Under it a simple "Say Yes" closed the ad.

"Great stories start with yes" had been substituted for something simpler, but the power of "Yes" remained. The most positive word you can say was victorious again. I now knew and was confident that I could repeat this trick with any brand and it would still work.

It does not matter if it's for Danonino, Kitkat or BMW. Saying "yes" is something that customers cannot fight against. I am not saying you should always use it (far from it), but it's a weapon that you can draw when you are stuck. The power of "yes" will be enough for your creative director to say "yes" to your idea, but do not expect him to say "yes" to a raise with that sort of idea. You are warned.

~

Chapter 13

The Art of...

THE ART OF…

> "Life is made up of repetitions."
> **Johan August Strindberg**

The art of being born; the art of growing up; the art of becoming a creative; the art of teaching; the art of learning; the art of learning to unlearn; the art of copying; the art of stealing; the art of writing a book called "Advertising Superpowers", etc…

Yes, there are many things you can do and many ways to do them, but none will be better done than with a touch of "art". Therefore, dear pals, work with passion, but don't forget to start using "the art of …" from time to time at the end of your campaign. Why? Because all your clients like to hear that their product is as lofty, important and imaginative as art.

So, without any meditation and any second thought, I will think about brands at random, and write "the art of …" as a tagline that best fits the product. Here I go:

Nike: The art of going beyond your limits.

Mercedes: The art of driving.

Swatch: The art of time.

Evian: The art of water.

Staedtler: The art of drawing.

Lego: The art of imagining.

Gillette: The art of shaving.

Playboy: The art of the nude.

Dove: The art of feeling beautiful.

Nintendo: The art of playing.

Coca-Cola: The art of happiness.

Starbucks: The art of starting the day right.

Kellog's: The art of starting the day right. (Yes, them too).

Gillette: The art of being a man.

Gillette: The art of being caressed by women.

UFC: The art of fighting.

Google: The art of making the world's information accessible.

Jameson Whiskey: The art of distilling.

Danonino: The art of growing healthy.

Heineken: The art of traveling the world.

Disney: The art of making you dream.

Red Bull: The art of flying.

Vodafone: The art of communicating.

Paypal: The art of paying.

Can you see how this works for every single brand?

I could do this all-day long. In fact, I will continue a little longer because I am having so much fun with it.

McDonalds: The art of making hamburgers that look like rubber.

Burger King: The art of making you believe that they are cooler than McDonalds.

Marlboro: The art of selling cigarettes with cowboys.

Apple: The art of selling computers with a fruit.

Pepsi: The art of never being convinced by their own logo.

Zara: The art of copying big brands and denying it.

Durex: The art of making you believe that sex is more pleasant with a condom on.

Bauhaus: The art of telling you that you can build the house of your dreams, through the ugliest ads.

Spotify: The art of making you pay for music that they have not produced.

Gucci: The art of being a luxury brand even when Cristiano Ronaldo dresses with their clothes from top to bottom.

I'm liking this so much! I think I have to be a bit more adventurous. I will continue this exercise of improvisation with the world of advertising. Not sure what the result will be but I have a funny feeling that this will be my favorite paragraph.

Cannes Lions: The art of selling Lions.

D&AD: The art of selling pencils as if they were Lions.

El Sol Festival: Same as above, but for Latin ads.

Miami Ad School: The art of teaching advertising creativity.

Other advertising schools: The art of imitating Miami Ad School.

Chief Creative Officer: The art of making clients believe that he or she is the most creative figure in the agency.

Executive Creative Director: The art of making people believe that he does not want to take the Chief Creative Officer's position.

Creative Director: The art of making people believe that the idea is his and not the creative team's.

Copy: The art of saying that the idea is his and not the Art Director's.

Art Director: The art of carrying the "Director" tag without really directing anything.

Trainees: The art of working without knowing if they are a copywriter or an art director yet.

And what about the accounts department? Let's see.

Account Directors: The art of believing that they are more important than the Creative Director and giving themselves permission to correct the art director, the copywriter and completely ignore the existence of the trainee.

Account Executives: The art of believing that they are more important than the Creative Director and giving themselves permission to correct the art director, the copywriter and the trainee whose name they never remember.

Account Supervisors: The art of believing that they are more important than the Creative Director and giving themselves permission to correct the art director, the copywriter and make the trainee believe that they are friends.

Accounts Trainee: The art of being the most annoying person to the creative department, as long as the Account Director, the Account Executive and the Account Supervisor are not around.

I would have liked to add the figure of the CEO and the Vice President, but for a lack of clarity in what they do, it is difficult to attribute to them the "art" of something other than "the art of working hard without anyone really knowing what they do".

As you can see, this works for all brands, and even for

people. I have found this exercise to be almost addictive. I will not continue though, since you can see how easy it is to generate a campaign tagline that will be loved by your client.

So, do not go crazy with that brief you hate. If you feel like going home early because your girlfriend has come to see you this weekend, or because she also is a creative and has miraculously managed to leave before 10.30pm, or you feel like leaving early because it is summaertime and you want to go back to the pub's terrace with your buddies without having to keep thinking incessantly on the brief, just add the "art of" to your idea and you'll be good to go.

Remember, your Executive Creative Director probably had the same idea to save his ass and went home a long time ago. The only difference is that they pay him five times what they pay you. Think about it.

~

Chapter 14.

CREATE CONFLICT WHATEVER it TAKES.

Donatella Versace

From everyone that had the patience to teach me to be an advertising creative, one piece of advice was repeated more than any other. Over and over again, I heard, "Santi, a good ad must have an insight".

For those who don't know the meaning of insight in the advertising context, it simply refers to the situations that are true in the consumers' mind. Like when you're watching 'Who Wants to be a Millionaire' and you guess the answer from the comfort of your home. Right there, your mom turns around, looks at you and proudly says, "You should go on that game show, my son".

Haven't we all experienced this situation? Many of us surely have. It instinctively feels familiar and it feels true. That makes it an insight. Something that we all believe to be true, whether it is or not.

What do I mean by that? Take this example. We know that if we see a banana peel on the floor in a commercial, someone will slip over on it. Have we ever seen someone trip over with one in real life? Probably not. But thanks to hundreds of cartoons and TV shows, we all universally recognize that a discarded banana peel is a shortcut to someone slipping over. Again, this is an insight.

After being constantly reminded on the importance of insights by my tutors, it might not come as a surprise to you that I spent years writing them down, hoping that I would find the great insight that would make me world famous.

However, during this exhaustive search for human truths, I discovered that my 'teachers' had not taught me the true secret of how to make great ads. I had only been taught part of it. Either they had deceived me or, they just didn't quite know the true secret that I am about to share with you.

Yes, ladies and gentlemen, for this alone, this book is worth buying.

Great ads do not have an insight. No. Great ads have two! That's right. Two conflicting truths that are revealed and live together inside your ad. All art, all movies, I would even dare to say all stories since the beginning of time have two opposing elements. Haven't you noticed?

Look around you. In religion, we have the conflict between good and evil, heaven and hell. Politics is a struggle for supremacy between the left and the right. In sport, the same thing happens. There would be no Federer without Nadal. No Barcelona without Real Madrid. In film, Batman would be flat boring without the Joker, and Rocky wouldn't manage to lift you off your seat if it wasn't for Apollo Creed. Conflicting elements can be found in us too. Think about the struggle between our right and left brain hemispheres, the fights that we go through in our decision making as our artistic side wrestles with our rational side. Conflicts are everywhere and they are what make things interesting.

So, now I have clarified this, let's jump into the world of advertising and see how this secret works in our beloved industry.

First of all, I'd like to remind everyone that advertising is not a science, so we cannot expect this formula to be present in every campaign. But a majority of winning ideas are built around a conflict of truths.

This is the formula and how it works:

TRUTH 1 vs. TRUTH 2 = CONFLICT

And the solution to this CONFLICT is the brand or product being advertised.

Let's see some proper examples to understand this better:

Harvey Nichols.

For their Christmas ad in 2014-2015, Harvey Nichols decided to play with two very powerful insights that we have all experienced. These truths helped them create a wonderful campaign that won several Grand Prix at the Cannes Lions Festival (Image 15).

The campaign I am talking about is the acclaimed "Sorry, I spent it on myself", which was built around the following formula:

> Truth 1: When I have money, I want to buy things for myself.
> Truth 2: When Christmas arrives, I must give gifts to others with my money.

By confronting these truths, a conflict ignites between the obligation to be generous and the desire to be selfish. A conflict that obviously becomes palpable throughout the ad.

What solves that conflict? As we've said previously, the brand or the product. In this case, Harvey-Nichols created a series of crappy gifts such as rubber bands, toothpicks and even a sink plug. All of them packaged with "Sorry, I spent it on myself". A way to be selfish, while still giving something (of sorts) to others at Christmas.

Image 15

Dove.

Dove has always seemed to understand the insights of the beauty industry better than their competitors. Over the last decade, they have consistently advocated for the need to feel confident no matter how you look. In their ad "Camera Shy", they demonstrated it in a masterful way.

As in the Harvey-Nichols ad, Dove created a TV spot that showed a conflict of truths, although they were presented in a completely different way.

> **Truth 1: Adult women are very concerned about their appearance and are insecure around cameras.**
>
> **Truth 2: When those same women were kids, they loved to be photographed and filmed.**

By confronting both truths, a struggle is generated between the insecurity of the adult woman and the carefree nature of her as a young girl.

The resulting campaign went something like this...

Image 16

We open with a series of vignettes of adult women who are desperately hiding from someone trying to video or take a photo of them in an unsuspecting way. One after the other, they look for ways to hide their faces from the camera, a little insecure in front of a camera (Image 16). After a few seconds, and after seeing dozens of women hiding from cameras, a title interrupts those images with the following message:

"When did you stop thinking you are beautiful?"

The question remains unanswered for a few seconds, until the ad reveals little girls aged 4–5 acting up for the camera proudly. The exact opposite way the grown adults did a moment ago. They do not hide from the camera but revel in showing off, enjoying being recorded and photographed.

Both moments are instantly familiar. Who likes having a camera shoved in their faces when they're not prepared? Not me. But give a child a chance to show off in front of a camera and they couldn't be happier. This clash of truths elevates the ad so much that it is hard to forget it once you have seen it.

Again, the formula "TRUTH 1 VS. TRUTH 2 = CONFLICT" works. What is the solution to the conflict? The brand of course when it invites you to "Be your beautiful self."

Atlético de Madrid.
Being Spanish, I did not want to miss the opportunity to show a Spanish example that uses conflict in its storytelling. The best example that I have found, probably my favorite Spanish campaign ever, is the ad featuring the first member of the Atlético de Madrid team.

It goes like this...

We hear the voice of a man who explains the aches and pains that come with age. He has been forced to quit pretty much everything he liked. "I quit tobacco and my coffee after every meal. I gave up salt, brandy, playing cards, betting and the other small pleasures of my life." But at the end, while watching television he releases a heartbreaking, "but not my damn Atleti". The image fades to black and right there, on our screen one of the most beautiful and universal taglines that have ever been created in advertising appears (Image 17):

"It kills me."

And a second later.

"It keeps me alive. Atlético de Madrid." (And it sounds even better in Spanish).

Image 17

Again, even with just a few words, we find that clash of truths that every sports fan knows.

Truth 1: Being a fan of a football club is hard. Watching them lose and find little success for years on end is heartbreaking. For fans, it 'kills' them.

Truth 2: Being a fan of football club gives you purpose, pride and hope. For fans, it gives them life.

There is no possible solution apart from continuing to live and remain a fan of the team. It does not matter if you are a fan or not of Atlético de Madrid. Any person who is passionate about something in life will understand.

This ad won a Bronze Lion a few years ago, personally I find it very little reward for such a sublime TV spot. Of course, we must be honest and realize that an international jury will not know what Atlético de Madrid represents. It's not Real Madrid or Manchester United. The number one member of Atlético de Madrid is nothing more than an old man nobody knows. But think for a minute if the same script was given to the Los Angeles Lakers team. The most famous team in the history of basketball, and think that instead of the unknown member of Atlético de Madrid, we take Jack Nicholson, who seems to be the most unconditional Lakers fan ever. In the twilight of his life, the famous actor tells how he has managed to overcome all his vices. Everyone, except his love for the Lakers because, 'They kill him. They keep him alive.' Had the ad been shot for the Lakers, we would now be talking about a Grand Prix winner at Cannes. 100%.

I hope you do realize that the formula gets repeated again and again. There are enough examples out there to write a whole book about them, but maybe it's good that you try to discover them by yourself and learn to recognize the structure.

To finish, it seems fair to clarify that I did not discover this magic advertising formula. I learnt it by observing ads with a microscope and by feeling the resulting tension created by conflicts. Also, I was lucky to work with a Brazilian Art Director called Atila Martins who had an analytical eye and explained to me why I felt butterflies in my stomach when I watched certain types of ads.

As a disclaimer, I would like to add that once you know the winning formula, you start looking for it in every book you read, every movie you watch and every story you are told.

You soon realize that every character has an internal battle or conflict. You watch an Apple presentation by Steve Jobs and see how he would never unveil a new product without creating a conflict or antagonism with other brands in the industry. As Steve declared, "the storyteller is the most powerful man in the world" and there is no one more powerful in advertising than the creative who knows how to tell stories with conflicts.

Unfortunately, I now have a professional distortion of the

way I look at ads, I can no longer enjoy any of them. I simply analyze TV spots to see if there is a conflict between truths. If there isn't one, the ad will soon be forgotten, but if a conflict appears, it will fill me with envy and strengthen my ego for I am able to see something that most creatives miss.

~

Chapter 15

WITHOUT TENSION YOU HAVE NOTHING.

> "In life, we love tranquility.
> In books, we love tension."
> **Ben Dolnick**

Nobody likes to feel tense. Whether it's because of stress or simply because it's cold outside, tension gives you that uncomfortable feeling of stiffness in the shoulders that forces you to shrink. But the tension we are about to discuss in this chapter has little to do with stress or cold. I talk about the tension that you feel when watching a movie, looking at a print ad or listening to a radio commercial.

In the previous chapter, we learnt how a contrast of truths provokes a clash between two feelings that are eventually resolved by the product or the brand. During this friction of truths, an element is created and is key in all forms of storytelling: tension.

All the arts use it. Music through changes of rhythm, introduction of new instruments, perfectly synchronized pauses, etc. TV shows by stopping for a commercial break just before they reveal if the contestant is about to become a millionaire or go home empty handed. In newspapers, the tension is in the striking headlines that make you want to read more. And in, every story is created with tension in mind. Well, with the exception of the Disaster Artist.

Let's take a look at movies and how they are constructed, since it gives an insight into how advertising tension works too. We've all seen Pixar movies, or at least we've heard about them. It turns out that the random funny stories imagined by the geniuses at Pixar aren't random at all. They use a very clear methodology that ensures that tension is generated throughout the film.

The magicians of Pixar call it the "the seven-step process". I discovered it by reading an excellent book called "The Storyteller's Secret from TED speakers to business legends" and watching videos on YouTube featuring a guy called Austin Madison; one of the animators and visual artist of movies like Ratatouille, WALL-E, Toy Story 3 and Brave.

Austin Madison unveils the keys for a successful script. For a Pixar movie to work, it must include the following 7 steps.

Once upon a time ____.
(A hero shares his goal. This is the most important element of the story.)

Every day, he / she _____.
(The heroes' life must be calm and monotonous in the first act.)

Until one day, _____.
(An absorbing story introduces a conflict/ tension, i.e. the hero faces a challenge that must be overcome.)

Because of that, _____.
(The tension builds as our hero faces the challenge. This step is critical and will determine if the movie becomes a blockbuster. Each scene should hook well with the previous and the next to create tension.)

Because of that, _____.
(The tension is ratcheted up some more.)

Until finally _____.
(At this point the victory of good over evil is revealed. The hero reaches the objective from point number 1).

Since then _____.
(The moral of the story)

Well, this simple process that seems to be written by my childish self is what has turned Pixar into a company valued at seven billion (yes, with a 'b') dollars. Seven steps to help the audience submerge in a story through conflicts and tension.

Just so that this makes a little more sense, and I hope you don't mind me indulging in my geeky side, I am going to use Star Wars to illustrate this structure:

1. **Once upon a time there was a farmer boy who wanted to be a pilot (Luke Skywalker).**

2. **Every day, he helped his uncle on the farm.**

3. **Until one day, his whole family is murdered and receives a message from Princess Leia.**

4. **Because of that, he joins the legendary Jedi Obi-Wan Kenobi.**

5. **Because of that, he hires Han Solo to take him to Alderaan.**

6. **Until, finally, Luke becomes a pilot and saves the mission / the planet.**

7. **Since then, Luke is fighting to become a Jedi Knight.**

You see, it's not a Pixar movie, but we see the same structure clearly repeated. Well, this structure (or similar) is used to tell stories in books, presentations, scripts, theater, journalism, etc. And all with the same purpose: to captivate the viewer through tension.

Knowing all this, our role as creatives should be to think about where / how / when we should introduce tension in our campaigns. We must look to see what elements can be altered or changed to add that little extra touch of tension, that additional silence, that little suspense that makes you go from shortlist to bronze, or from bronze to gold.

To illustrate how it's done in advertising I would like to share a few print campaigns that were created at Young & Rubicam (Prague), where I used to work. When you think of this agency, you do not associate it with creative greatness. And even when you work there, you still don't associate with it.

However, year after year, with little budgets and no help from elsewhere, we were able to win Lions at the Cannes festival. This small agency managed to lift about 15 lions and more than 40 shortlists in 3 years, whilst many bigger agencies with more money and logistics can't scrape together a single shortlist, no matter how hard they try. What is the key to this success in Prague? Well, they understand the power of tension in storytelling, and how this element can better any campaign you have come up with.

The first time I heard about it was when the guys at Young & Rubicam shared with me how they created the most awarded piece from the agency: a series of prints for Harley-Davidson that won Gold or Grand Prix in 90% of the advertising festivals they were presented to. Since the story of how they came up with this campaign is as wonderful as the print ads themselves, it is my duty to share it with all of you.

Back in 2009, a guy called Conor Barry, copywriter in Y&R Prague at the time, reads a story about the Second World War in the newspaper. The article talks about a few Czech riders who dismantled their Harley-Davidsons and hid the pieces between household objects so that when the Nazis raided the homes, they could not recognize the parts of those bikes and confiscate them to continue financing the Nazi war. Their hope was that one day, the conflict would end and they could reassemble their bikes to return them to the roads.

Without a doubt, it is a unique and incredible story that deserved to be told and shared with the world, even if it's through an ad. At that point, the Chief Creative Officer, Jaime Mandelbaum, decided to let anyone in the agency come up with a creative solution to transform this story into a winning piece of advertising. Despite hearing loads of different ideas, it was four years until he gave an idea his blessing. My partner Atila Martins found the light at the end of the tunnel. No need to say that the visuals he came up with were full of tension, and made the ad worth of two Gold Lions in Cannes.

The campaign itself was composed of 4 print ads shot from the POV of the dismantled Harley pieces (Image 18). In each of

WITHOUT TENSION, YOU HAVE NOTHING

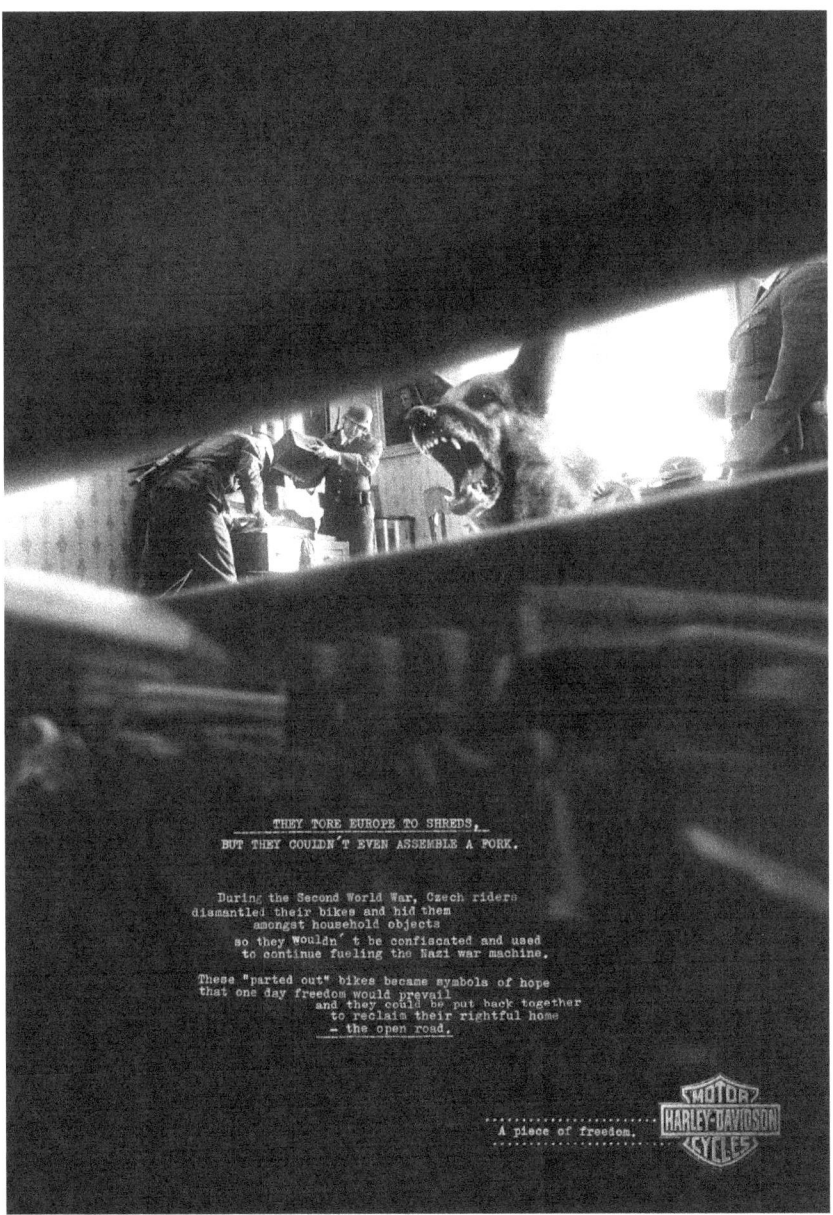

Image 18

the ads, a house is being raided by Nazis who are in search of reusable material. The proximity of a dangerous barking dog, a sergeant looking directly into the hole where the piece is hidden, etc. provides the tension. Expertly captured in the photographs, they make the viewer uncomfortable, just like the owners of the Harley's would have been. The copy from the ad is also majestic. Some of the best I have ever read. It's got rhythm and the same tension that you feel with the visuals. You know what? Here it is so you can judge by yourself.

"During the Second World War, Czech riders dismantled their bikes and hid them amongst household objects so they wouldn't be confiscated and used to continue fueling the Nazi war machine. These "parted out" bikes became symbols of hope that one day freedom would prevail and they could be put back together to reclaim their rightful home—the open road. Harley Davidson. A piece of Freedom."

The following year we wanted to do a sequel, but the story we relied on was not as nice. Aware of the success we had achieved by relying on tension, our main focus was to create as much as possible this time around. In the example, you can see a Nazi soldier lying on the floor crying at the imminent arrival of the Allied army that is about to liberate the city of Pilsen (Image 19).

This series of print ads is another example of how to use

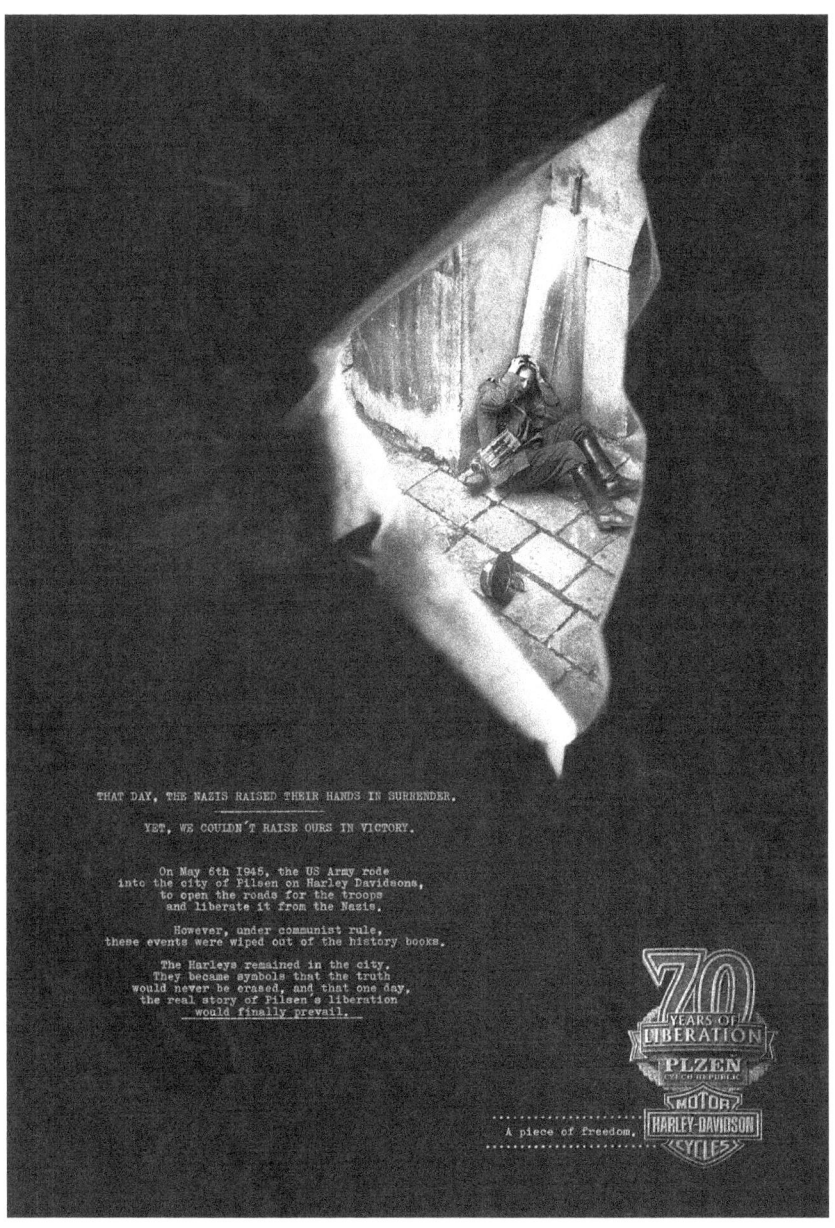

Image 19

tension to impact the viewer. Although the pictures are definitely not as good, the headlines worse, and the text a little clumsier, the feeling the ad gives you is similar to the year before, and that was enough to take two more Bronze Lions for the agency, some virtual patting on the back for me and a raise for my boss.

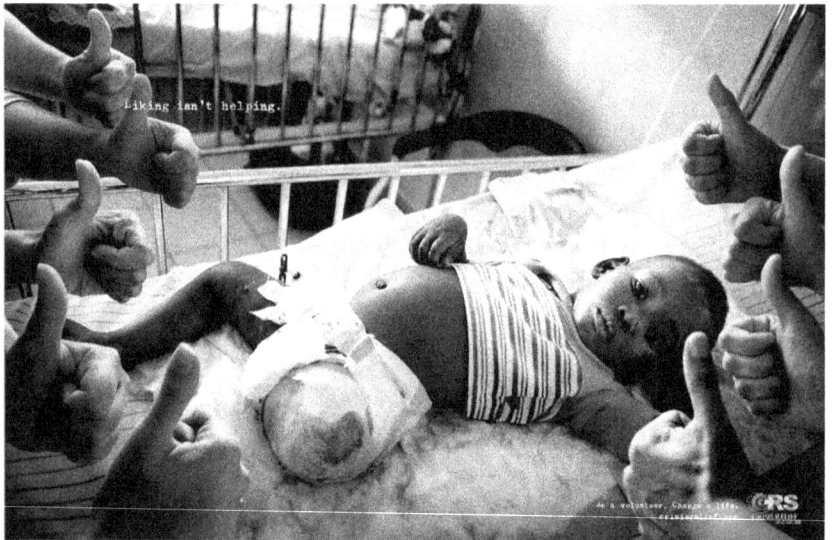

Image 20

Crisis Relief.

Another example of remarkable tension is that of the Crisis Relief print ads. In this campaign, we see realistic looking scenes of war zones. In the image, a mother is holding her son who is gasping for air, and about to die in her arms. Around them, we can see a bunch of thumbs up which imitate "likes" in social networks (Image 20).

By contrasting these opposing realities (Internet vs the Third World), the authors are able to produce a feeling of creepiness that leaves no one apathetic. My personal opinion is that it's not necessary to resort to such harsh images for an advertising campaign, but still the ad works perfectly. Better than most. Why? It has tension.

Image 21

Freddo ice cream.

Freddo is a brand which releases some great looking ads almost every year. In this case, the creative team decided to play with the "extreme" love a kid can feel for an ice cream. In them, we discover children twisted in impossible positions after an unfortunate fall doing everything humanly possible to save their Freddo ice cream (Image 21).

The pictures are taken at a moment of maximum tension, when you don't know if the kids are trapped or if they will be able to move and save their Freddo. What you did know is what would happen to this ad in Cannes. It was destined to only one outcome: a Gold Lion. Why? Tension.

Image 22

Sunlight

Finally let's look at this fun print campaign for Sunlight which breathes tension in a totally different way. The campaign is made up of three magnificently retouched print ads where a pig, a sheep and a cow cling desperately to the pan or dish where they have supposedly been consumed. Thanks to the product, a dishwashing liquid it is possible to separate the "food" from the dish in a heartbeat (Image 22).

    This campaign also won a Gold Lion in Cannes. Do you still think it's a coincidence? I don't think so. All these campaigns have one thing in common. You know what it is.

~

Chapter 16

Go Literal, not Lateral.

> "There's more than one way to skin a cat."
> **No idea who came up with this sentence**

Dear creatives,

The time has come to speak of one of the most overused and hated tricks in the history of advertising: stupid visual puns. A visual that literally depicts a common phrase or expression. If you're not sure what I mean yet, you will in a second (and I promise you won't like it). It's a trick despised by most creatives, but surprisingly loved by far too many clients.

It does not matter if you work in Croatia, New York or Madrid. Every creative from the most unknown to the one and only David Droga (an advertising superstar if you don't know him yet) has considered taking a famous phrase and visualizing it literally.

But let me give you some horrendous examples (apologies if they cause you to vomit uncontrollably into your mouth). I have decided to keep the identity of the creatives secret as to not provoke mighty revenge. And also, because we have all succumbed to the use of going literal. Me too. More than once…

For a car brand.

A few years ago, a Spanish advertising agency, whose name I will not share, decided to send to Cannes an ad with less chance of winning a lion than any other ever submitted in the history of advertising. It went like this: a man enters a car dealership and asks for a quote. The seller informs him of the price and then the client, amazed by what he just heard, starts to look everywhere in the store. He looks over the shoulder of the car seller, he looks under the car, he looks in the trash can. It goes on and on. Meanwhile, the salesman stares at him with a puzzled face. Finally, we understand what the "joke" was as the voice over says: "A price that you will not find anywhere else". Ouch! You won't find that price anywhere, so I present someone searching for that price like a Muppet.

For a bank.

In English, we all know that "Bill" is both the name of a person and the annoying letters that claim some of your hard-earned money. So, a certain bank took the Bill thing literally and created the following ad. A man goes to pick up his mail. But instead of the mail there's a huge man called Bill in his mailbox. The voice over said something along the lines of "Nobody likes to receive a Big Bill".

For a telephone company.

For a campaign, a certain international telephone company decided to run an ad with a photograph of a giant Converse shoe alongside the headline, "Have longer conversations." Being in Prague and not speaking the Czech language, I could not understand what a Converse sneaker had to do with calling someone. After double-checking with my colleagues, it turned out that the word "conversation" is similar in Czech to "Converse". So, there you had the image of a red converse shoe, accompanied by a 'smart' headline that invited you to have longer "conversations". Okay, I get it! Thanks for putting that ad directly in eyeline of my office. And not changing it for a year. Every day, day-in day-out, I had to look at that crappy pun.

Should I stop? It's getting to me.

From my point of view, this is the lowest form of advertising. The crappiest and stingiest form of coming up with ideas that requires no creativity whatsoever (we're called 'creatives' for a reason). So, whilst it's true that on some occasions it raises a smile, the result is always a dumb ad that you will undoubtedly feel ashamed of sharing with your mates. Even your mum.

These crap puns have become a very common resource that creatives use when they are stuck and have to show something to their supervisor. For some reason, they are also often used in self-promotion campaigns for junior creative teams. Proof more often than not, that the team doing the self-promotion isn't very creative at all.

Here are a few uncreative examples from creative teams. Of course, they ended up looking silly and in most cases, not getting a job.

Let's start off with the grave. A creative team decided to send an actual grave to the Chief Creative Officer of one of the most awarded advertising agencies in Madrid (the creatives behind "Justino") along with the line "we are dying to work in your agency". The first thing that comes to mind when you think of that phrase is dead people, cemeteries, and graves. I guess a grave was the easiest literal execution they could produce (Image 23). Truly dying to get a job would have been a little extreme. The "gift" was received with laughter by the CCO and he even shared a picture with his social network. But that's about how much the creative team got out of that idea. A tiny bit of exposure, a smile (at their expense) and a quick "no, thank you".

Another example is the guy who sent a kidney to a Creative Director, with the line: "I would give a kidney to work with you". He went literal with his execution and showed zero creativity. Needless to say, he didn't get the job either.

Image 23

In similar fashion (Image 24) a couple of Czech creatives were distributing bags of blood (allegedly from themselves) to every Prague advertising agency with the line; "Your agency needs fresh blood". The promo campaign was pretty neatly executed but again, a literal execution resulted in no job offers for them either.

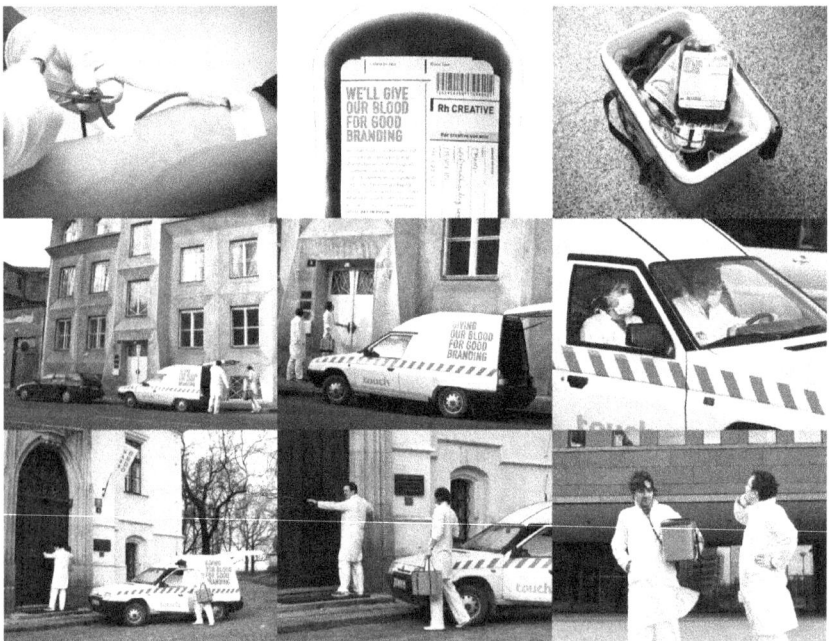

Image 24

In England, a young and very stubborn man decided to take the expression "put a foot in the door" literally. He built a giant foot that he pushed through the city to various agencies. When he arrived, he literally pushed his foot in the door. They are many videos of this stunt and the reactions could not be more different. He was received with laughter in some cases, and others pretty much told him to "get the f*** out of here". Finally, after a few months of dragging his giant foot around the city of London, an agency considered that, although his portfolio wasn't up to scratch, his attitude and perseverance were worth a chance. Good for him.

We could go on all day and talk about hundreds of other examples of ads where you execute things literally. But there's no need to share any others. I think I have inflicted enough pain upon you already.

Yes, this trick can get you out of trouble in a hurry when you're stuck, but it is better to avoid it. And, above all, when your creative director says to one of your ideas, "give it a twist". Don't take that opportunity to record yourself turning and twisting the idea pad in your hand. It's just not funny.

Whether you use this literal trick or not is up to you, but certainly, if you are very desperate and want to find inspiring phrases for your next campaign, a small search on the internet will give you much more than you need.

~

Chapter 17

DONATE YOUR MUM.

William S. Burroughs

For a few years now, campaigns no longer talk about the product features. In fact, they do not even talk about the product. Whether they are an NGO or a lollipop brand, they are more likely to tell you how the product is helping to save the world, end climate change, empower millennials or save lives. They all seem to find a place from where to add to the apocalypse of goodness that has flooded advertising. I confess, I have been among those who have collaborated in feeding this "monster". When there is a trend, sometimes you can't help but follow it. So, if you have to help some homeless people to win an award, I mean to save a life, then you should do it.

We must save lives. We must do good. We must donate. Donate whatever. Don't believe me? Search "donation campaigns" on Google and you will find things like: donate your data, your hair, your voice, your calories, your blood, your kidneys, your old shoes, your car, your shadow, your Wi-Fi, the minutes that are left over from your mobile, a word, your hate, your Facebook status... Whatever. The point is that you must donate, donate and donate, and do good.

Now seriously, how far are we going to go with this "I have to do good with my brand"?

Any of us who work in advertising know that in recent years the number of socially motivated campaigns has increased so much so that they now dominate at award shows. You're more likely to be awarded for savings lives than selling products. So now all brands follow the same pattern: I will "do good", people will buy me, I will feel good. All creatives follow the same pattern: I will "do good", people will give me an award at some local festival, I will feel good. But so much goodness is sometimes nauseating, not because of how it is done, but for the reason it is done. We are wolves in sheep's clothing. 'Save the seals!' we shout as we sneakily sell you dishwashing liquid. But what we are really saying is "Guys, I know I interrupt people with my ads, but I'm trying to do good this time. You wouldn't have a Lion for me, would you?"

What are our true intentions? Do we still care for the plight of the people our campaigns 'help' the second we finish our case studies? Are we really saving lives or playing with them to satiate our own vanity? Do you not miss the not so distant times when ads weren't afraid to just sell stuff? Those campaigns that presented a product in a way that nobody had thought of before and people commended it simply because it was fun or original or smart. Am I the only one who yearns for that time? I don't know. I doubt it. But as I said, I am also one of the contributors to this identity crisis that advertising is facing.

But it's not worth complaining about. Because in this industry, as I have said before, what you are not willing to do, another will without second thought. So, let's accept how this is and instead of changing things, let's use them to our advantage. We are here to learn how and where to get ideas from. In this case, it's easy, just look around to see what problem you find and try to solve it with your brand. In the last year, the industry has been flooded by campaigns that talk about gender equality for instance. Open your eyes for new trends to come. But first, let's look at some examples.

Recycling.
Volkswagen's "Fun Theory" was a campaign initially created to demonstrate how fun can change people's behavior and push them to do things they normally feel lazy about—like recycling or putting their trash in the bin. The idea was presented to VW who rejected it because it had nothing to do with their cars. But then, the creators of the Fun Theory decided to post the videos anyway. The positivity and simplicity of the videos struck audiences around the world and the Fun Theory went viral. They became an instant hit.

Seeing the success of the campaign, VW suddenly became very interested in continuing the campaign. They didn't roll out a big recycling program or initiative, they just made more ads. Proof that brands don't care that much about saving the world, they care more about making something that consumers love, and if that means making consumers falsely think they care about the environment, so be it. I still like my VW Polo though.

Homeless.

If recycling is not your thing, look around. The streets, unfortunately, are full of homeless people. For a long time, using them in campaigns had become a sort of trend. Yes, there are trends in advertising, and homelessness was one of them.

Image 25

There are countless examples of campaigns that confirm what I am saying. The best I remember has to be "Fuck the Poor".

On a seemingly normal day in London, a boy stands in the middle of a busy street asking for money for the poor. His way of doing it is somehow strange, as he shouts out "Fuck the poor!" in the face of passers-by who cannot help but be outraged (Image 25). Some of these confrontations get extremely tense and you worry about the safety of the man. During the video, a slide shows the following message: "We know that you care about the poor."

In a magnificent twist, we now see the same man in the same street, only a few minutes later. But now he's simply shouting, "Help the poor", while rattling his empty donation tin. And what do you think happens? Well nobody even looks at him. He is completely ignored, as if he was invisible. Do people really care as much as they say?

There's been hundreds of campaigns supporting the homeless, many of them play with the cardboard sign that homeless use to ask for help. One of them for Impact Homelessness created a campaign called "Rethink" (Image 26).

In it, they replaced the usual messages the homeless write with an unexpected truth about their past lives. Thus, we saw a girl living in the street holding a sign that read, "Previously,

I was an artistic figure skater". Another example was a man holding a sign, "I speak 4 languages". A chilling way to make you see that many lives just as normal as yours end up on the street.

Image 26

In Spain, similar campaigns have also been made, although they seem a little more trivial. An example is the Homeless Fonts campaign, in which the agency The Cyranos (without the Bergerac) created typography based on the writing of the Homeless (Image 27). This way, "Loraine's handwriting" became a typeface that you could buy and the money went to these homeless people. A nice stunt, but one that has more impact in festivals than it has in real life. It's just an opinion. No, it is not. I am right!

Image 27

Football

If you're not into recycling or homeless campaigns, as a creative you have an opportunity with the number one sport in the world: football. From Brazil, we have received thousands of campaigns that make football the savior of the planet, even if it was for a few weeks, days or even hours. With the use of a ball or a match they have managed to solve every social problem in recent years.

Blood donation: Official player shirts that would only get their original red stripes back if fans donated enough blood before the matches.

Organ donation: Ogilvy Brazil created the acclaimed "Immortal Fans" campaign in which Recife supporters could become donors and help people who needed an organ. This way, their passion for the team "would last" through their donated organs in the body of another person.

Domestic violence: Again, Ogilvy Brazil, the king of social campaigns, created "Security Moms", in which the mothers of the most violent fans became the football grounds security team during a game. The match was uneventful, because no one fights in front of their mother even if they are dangerous hooligans.

Unfortunately (or fortunately for some), the world is a little chaotic and there are many social causes that you can leverage for your advertising campaign: domestic violence, poor health, the extinction of animals, the cleanliness of the oceans, poverty, etc... I do not see anything wrong in doing it. I just hope you do it for the right reasons: to help. Not to increase your chances of winning awards.

In any case, what I say does not matter, because for now, advertising will continue with the same pattern: when a brand does not know what to communicate, a social campaign will follow. So, donate donate donate, and if you can, donate your mum. I personally don't have the guts to do it. But make no mistake, this is advertising, and what I do not dare to do, another will very soon. It's only matter of time. You wait and see! (sorry mums).

Chapter 18

PRESSURE HELPS.

> "There is no such thing as talent. There is pressure."
> **Alfred Adler**

The truth is, if you could choose, you'd rather work from the comfort of your home, a beer in hand while some music plays in the background. You would also love it if your boss favored a good working environment, if he'd let you do things the way you like and if he was patient, gentle and charming even when he didn't like your ideas.

It might seem crazy what I'm about to say, but although the above scenario may seem ideal at first and many will agree, my experience tells me otherwise. When I have been given room, space and freedom to operate, when I have been given a long time to think of ideas, like two weeks for a miserable couple of radio ads, the truth is that very little has come out of my brain. In fact, the lack of pressure caused the opposite effect to the desired one. Instead of coming up with brilliant polished ideas, all I could offer were rancid things that sounded just as boring as campaigns we've heard a hundred thousand times.

I remember perfectly when I was working in Paris at a leading agency under the command of a dictator who simply did not know how to talk to people without shouting. On paper, it was clearly the worst environment for a person to create freely. The pressure was unsustainable and we were all scared that this boss would stop us in the corridors or in the canteen where without any warning he would proceed to humiliate you in front of everyone. There was even a joke about it in the agency. When you were told off by him for the first time, people congratulated you for officially being "baptized".

Surprisingly, in that horrible environment, amazing campaigns came out one after another. Every pitch we entered, we won. I could not win a pitch in my previous agency even if there was no other agency competing for that client. Now I would find myself in an agency where in the course of six intense months, we won accounts like Meetic Europe, Pantene Middle East, Virgin Mobile, Burger King, Clarins, Nivea, Mondelez and more.

What was the key to such brilliance? On the one hand, it is necessary to recognize the merit and the selling skills of the bosses, but it is obvious that in order to sell an idea that idea must be good. So, how were we able to get good ideas in such a bad environment? Well, simply put, because as much as you dislike it, pressure helps you. If you manage to control it, it plays in your favor.

I remember a week in which we were really against the ropes. I was working on the latest Tipp-Ex campaign with Pharrell Williams, producing it swiftly so that it could be released and sent to Cannes that year. I was on my own, since my copywriter had left the agency as we started production. In some ways, I was doing the job of two people when even two were not enough at the frantic pace we operated. In those circumstances, the last thing I needed was for the agency to give me another brief to work on. But just as I was smoking yet another cigarette which seemed my only escape to the outside world, a colleague from the accounts department came to see me, and shared a brief for Meetic, our new client.

I remember I had been given a week to think of ideas. In any other situation one week would have been more than enough. But that week wasn't a normal one. I was producing my biggest campaign to date, a digital experience in five different languages that the world could participate in. On my own, desperate, I decided to concentrate on my Tipp-ex campaign and forget about Meetic.

In my mind I thought, "when the moment of presenting ideas comes, I'll simply tell the boss that I have a lot of work for Tipp-Ex and that I have no time to think about Meetic". But of course, that boss was not any boss, and if they had given me that brief it was because he had decided so. Therefore, when I told him about the situation the day before presentation, he replied that we had a meeting in less than 24 hours and that he expected me to come up with several good ideas.

I must admit that I panicked a bit. I had no longer seven days to think but less than a day. At this point I had two options: one was to stay in the office until very late even though I was so tired than words cannot begin to explain how I felt; the other possibility was to go home, rest and disappear from the agency in the morning to avoid any interruptions. That way I thought, I could get a good 2-3 hours of "quality" thinking. In the end, my body decided that if I ever was going to be able to think, I would need to rest first. So, I opted for going home and sleeping as much as I could under those circumstances.

What happened the next day, I will never forget.

I got up at eight. I showered and went to a Parisian bistro with a view of the "Galeries Lafayette". I started thinking knowing that I had a few hours to get ideas, before going into that room with the Dictator, the Vice-President, the Account Director, the Assistant Director and the Secretary. Five pairs of eyes staring and waiting for me to mess up so that I would give the Dictator something to shatter my self-esteem with. I have no explanation as to why, but that morning, the morning when I felt the most pressure in my creative life became the one in which I had the most productive three hours of my career.

Ideas came out without any effort. Insights floated through my mind constantly. The more I watched the clock tick the more ideas came out. In just a couple of hours I had at least four solid ideas that I liked, so instead of continuing to search for more, I spent the rest of the morning polishing them, writing them well and making them as clear as possible for the presentation.

When the time for the meeting arrived, not only did I no longer feel pressure, but I felt a desire to enter that room and demonstrate how I solved that brief by myself in such a short period of time. When they asked, who wanted to go first, while everyone was hiding, I shouted "I do" and I entered the boss's office with an unusual sense of confidence.

One by one, I shared my ideas with the bosses and I will never forget the smile they showed when they heard the quality of these. They liked them so much that they presented three of them to the client. Something completely unheard of in the agency. There were three other teams working on that brief for a full week. None of their ideas got selected.

That was the most discomforting week of my life, but one where I learned a great lesson: pressure is not the enemy of creativity, it is an ally. Don't feel scared about pressure, embrace it. Learn to manage it, use it to your advantage, and it will help you get the best out of you.

Since that day in Paris, I sometimes willingly wait until the last moment to start thinking of ideas. It's a dangerous way to live, but my experience tells me that the more pressure I feel, the better ideas come out of me.

~

Chapter 19

SIMPLY SIMPLIFY.

> "Complicating is easy.
> Simplifying is harder."
> **Max Gehringer**

I'm sure you have already heard of the acronym KISS. I do not mean the 80's glam rock band whose bassist's tongue could stretch down to his nipples. I am referring to the expression "Keep It Simple, Stupid". Although nobody agrees on whether the last "S" means stupid or something else, the point is that we are better off keeping things simple.

When you look at the great public speakers and orators of our time, you realize that they understand this premise better than anyone else. When they give a presentation, they know the importance of synthesizing so that their message is simple and easily understood.

As a big Steve Jobs fan, I would like to take this opportunity to comment on how he understood better than anyone the power of storytelling and the importance of summarizing your idea in one short sentence.

According to those who worked at Apple, Steve Jobs paralyzed the entire company for a month to prepare for the keynote presentation of a new product. It is no surprise that when you saw him on stage, everything he did seemed effortless. Steve Jobs presented his new products in front of large crowds. Mainly journalists and bloggers who would be writing articles in real time about Apple's new products. Jobs' acumen was such that during the course of his presentation he would always find a way to not only get his idea across in one sentence, but to deliver the headline he wanted journalists to write in their publications.

These are some of the greatest examples of how Steve Jobs sold the world his products in one sentence.

"Apple reinvents the phone" for the launch of the iPhone.

"1000 songs in your pocket" for the launch of the iPod.

"The world's thinnest notebook" for the launch of Macbook Air.

Rarely has someone been able to tell the value of a product or idea so easily and memorably. It might seem simple, but in reality, it is extremely hard.

Another example of the importance of simplifying your idea is the story of how Google was funded. Michael Moritz, a former editor of Time magazine, now a billionaire startup investor, explained how he met Larry Page and Sergey Brin and why he decided to invest in them. At Sequoia capital, Moritz saw about 70 projects per week and had to decide whether or not to invest in them within minutes. Often, he was frustrated that the ideas were not communicated simply to him, so he didn't understand the product he was being sold and therefore could not make up his mind about investing or not. People were showing a natural tendency to complicate things, but not Larry and Sergey. When they pitched in his office, Moritz was convinced to invest instantly. The moment he was told one simple sentence that explained what Google was for:

"We organize the world information, and make accessible."

That's it. Upon hearing that, the Sequoia capital CEO had no doubt that he should invest in them. The rest is history.

But let's go back to the world of advertising. In some way, we are trying to do exactly what Larry and Sergey did: explaining the benefit of the product or brand as simply as possible. To keep things brutally and beautifully simple.

As an advertising creative, I have often done the complete opposite. Unfortunately, that desire to embellish unnecessarily often resulted in a lack of interest from my teachers and bosses. For good reason.

When you look a little closer, you realize that most of the great ads of the last decade have one thing in common.

They start with a simple idea and can be easily told in one sentence.

Beauty Sketches, Dove:
Portraits that compare how women see themselves vs how others see them.

Holograms for freedom, We are not a crime:
The first hologram protest in history.

Inglorious Fruits and Vegetables, Intermarché:
Sell "ugly" fruits and vegetables to show that they are just as good as beautiful ones.

The Gun Shop, United States to Prevent Gun Violence:
A store that sells second-hand weapons that have been used in gun-crime.

Climate Name Change, Change.org:
Start naming hurricanes after the politicians who deny climate change.

Lifepaint, Volvo:
Spray paint that reflects in the dark to protect cyclists on the road.

Meet Graham, Transport Accident Commission:
A representation of how a human would look if they were designed to survive a car crash.

Scariest BK, Burger King:
Burger King disguises itself as Mcdonald's for Halloween.

McWhopper, Burger King:
A Big Mac and Whopper burger united for world peace.

Safety Truck, Samsung:
A rear screen on trucks to help cars overtake.

The salt you can see, Fundación Favaloro:
Colored salt that is visible in your food, so you can avoid excessive salt consumption.

The freshest orange juice, Intermarché:
Orange juice bottles labelled with the time the juice was made.

Pay per laugh, Teatreneu:
The first theater in which you pay depending on how much you laugh.

Price on the Jersey, Walmart:
Using the shirt number of soccer players to advertise product prices.

We could go on for hours and hours. All these campaigns

are winners of multiple awards and they all one thing in common: an idea so simple that it can be told in one sentence. For the idea to see the light, it needs to be original and brilliant too. You could not sell a simple idea if it was rubbish, but simplicity is always the way to go.

As a former advertising student turned advertising teacher, I have seen the opposite many times. There seems to be a force that makes us complicate our ideas so they seem bigger. We love to add elements but more often than not, the resulting campaigns lack effectiveness. Less is more and more is more of a mess. So just find a simple idea and please, tell it simply.

~

Chapter 20

Make them curious, show a benefit, or stand out.

Albert Camus

Due to the number of ads we see every day, getting customers interested in our products is increasingly difficult. So, how do you know in advance, if your ad has a chance of working?

The best thing to do is to be honest with yourself. Deep down you know if your work is good or if it's not. Generally speaking, when your idea is worth it, you feel something inside of you. However, if you have problems connecting with your gut feeling, my advice is to let your idea rest for a day. If after that period, you still think that your idea is worth it, it probably is, and you should move forward with it.

The problem is that if you are like me, this feeling of uncertainty is rather constant. You are never really sure of your idea that much. I believe that most creative people will agree on this. We are a bunch of fragile and insecure humans that carry our doubts with us everywhere, even if we have won hundreds of awards and have made the headlines several times. In fact, the best creatives I've met, the most talented, are probably also the most insecure. So, with such existential doubts, how can we find a way to know if our ad is right or not?

Well, even if it is probably not the only solution, I recommend you use a simple test that should help you know if your ad is good enough. When in doubt, ask yourself the following: Does my ad draw attention? Does my ad show a benefit? Does my ad create curiosity? If your campaign does all three, you probably have a great piece of work, regardless of what unfair criticisms might say. In fact, even if you meet only one of these three requirements, you already have a valid idea.

To demonstrate what I say, I would like to pay tribute to some advertising print ads that, despite requiring very little executional work, manage to fully meet the points mentioned in the previous paragraphs.

Does it draw attention?
To illustrate this point, I have selected a wonderful print campaign created for the "Cancer Patients Aid Association" by the agency Ogilvy & Mather Mumbai in 2009 (Image 28).

The simplest of layouts. Three words on a blank piece of paper that are enough to draw attention and highlight the benefit of the product:

"Cancer cures smoking."

A little play on words that hits you in the chest, and makes you feel proud to call yourself a creative. The sentence is cruel and harsh. The impact is not caused by the words they use but rather because of how they use them. Such a short sentence is hard to forget. Sometimes great advertising can be reduced to something as simple as this.

Does it show a benefit?
In an ideal world, every ad should show the benefit of buying a product. Makes sense, right? If you don't know what's in it for you why should you buy it? Surprisingly enough, many of the products that we see and consume on a daily basis do not have a benefit, so what do we do in these cases? You invent one. That simple. Just as the guys who worked for The Economist magazine have been doing for nearly three decades.

In one of their most memorable executions, created in 1984 by David Abbott, we see once again the power of a well-written headline.

The ad, just simple typography on an Economist red background (Image 29).

"I never read The Economist."
Management trainee. Aged 42

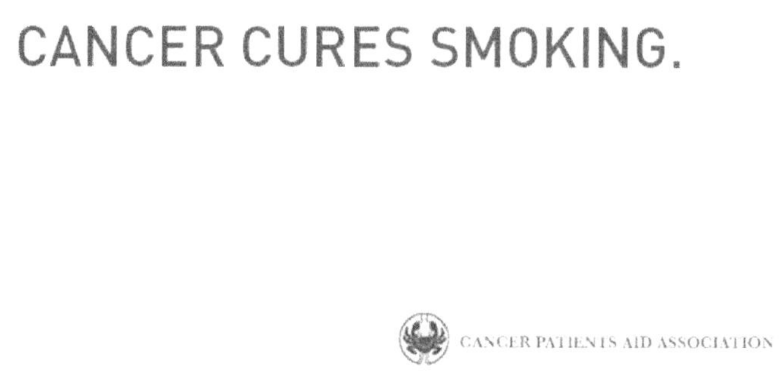
CANCER CURES SMOKING.
CANCER PATIENTS AID ASSOCIATION

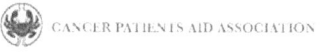

Image 28

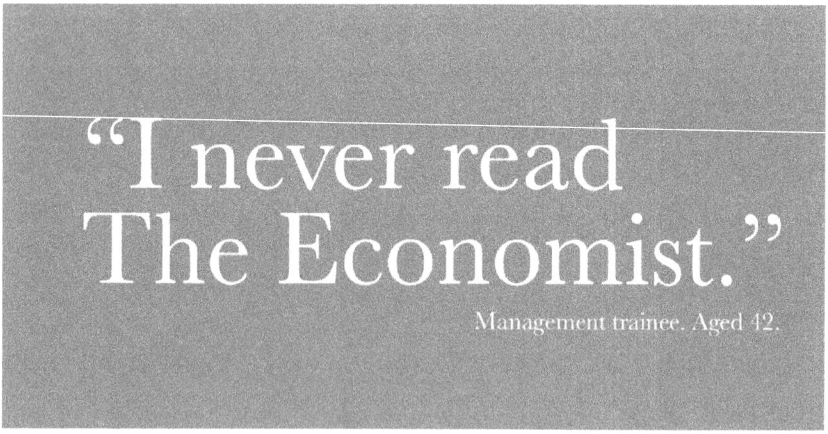
"I never read The Economist."
Management trainee. Aged 42.

Image 29

With a short quote and a signature, the benefit of reading the famous magazine is clear: good business people read The Economist. Unsuccessful people don't.

Is the benefit of reading The Economist real? Well, there might be some truth to it, but it is clearly taken to an extreme to get people's attention. A great ad and one the most acclaimed ever.

Another example of how to show a benefit is the wonderful job that the guys at JWT NY did years ago for the DeBeers jewelry brand. Using a playful as well as honest tone, they managed to make the male audience understand the 'enormous' benefit of buying one of their pieces of jewelry for their partner (Image 30).

One of the print ads shows an elegant diamond ring alongside the copy: "Getting rid of headaches since 1888".

A simple headline that any grown-up will understand and chuckle at. The consumer is made to understand that buying a diamond for your wife will not only make her happy, but that she will be eternally grateful. With a diamond in her hand, those nights spent sleeping on the sofa are gone, the complaints about watching football with the lads are over, and untimely nocturnal headaches that stop you from having sex with her will not be a problem anymore. Buy Debeers my friends.

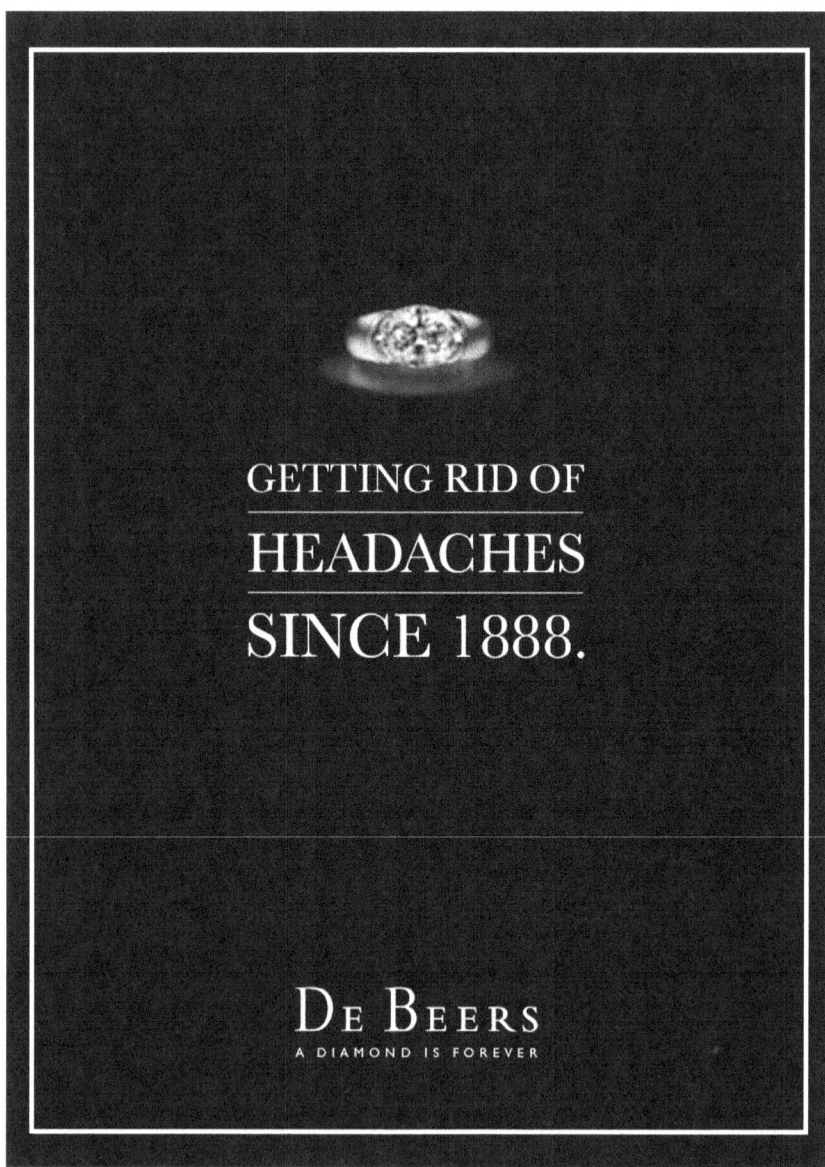

Image 30

MAKE THEM CURIOUS, SHOW A BENEFIT, OR STAND OUT

Does it make you curious?

Creating curiosity can be done in many different ways. You can do it with headlines, a word or with a strong image. Whatever works for the idea.

Not long ago, I remember seeing a campaign that was impossible not to feel curious about. In the ad, we see the torso of a woman about to slowly unbutton her blouse. Despite being exposed to constant images of nudity in today's world, one seems to never get enough of them. So, there I was on Facebook, clicking on my very first banner in over a decade.

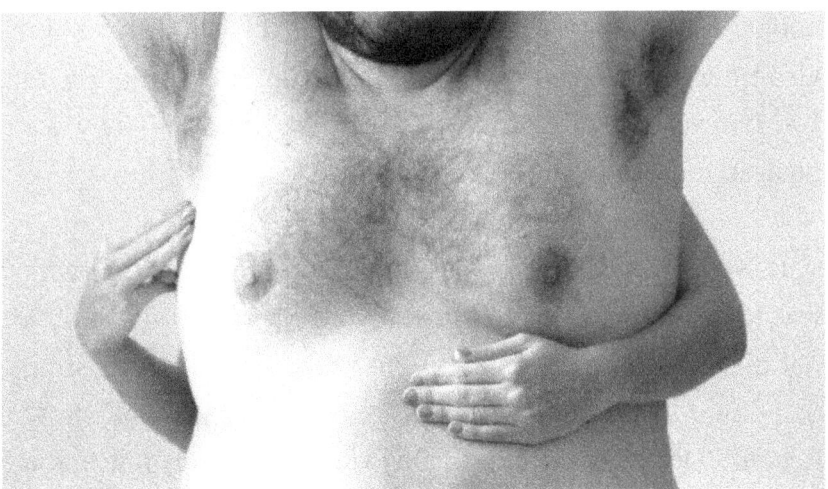

Image 31

No question that I was curious to see more. But what I saw, did not resemble what I expected at all. Actually, it was way better. Right at the moment when the girl was finally going to flash her breasts, she disappeared (nudity is banned on Facebook) and came back hiding behind an obese lad with a pair of very large man boobs (Image 31).

The girl stood behind him, and together, they performed a breast checkup to explain how to detect breast cancer. As a picture is worth a tale of a thousand words, see the visual attached and you will get a clearer idea of why most people would share the ad.

Needless to say, this campaign spread like wildfire. The very day of its launch, my Facebook wall was full of man boobs. A clear sign that most of my advertising mates were also interested in seeing boobs. If they are anything like me, I am sure, that after the initial disappointment, they were pleased to have been the victims of a very good ad.

In short, and getting back to the point of all this, which was to develop criteria to know if your idea is good or not. Do not hesitate to be self-critical, just ask yourself three simple questions: Does my ad draw attention? Does my ad show a benefit? Does my ad create curiosity? If you do not answer positively any of these three questions, then I am afraid that you should keep thinking about new ideas, because what you have will not interest anyone. Not even your mom.

~

Chapter 21

Don't believe in yourself, BUT BELIEVE IN YOUR IDEA.

> "It is good for men to believe in their ideas and to die for them."
> **Jean Anouilh**

If you have made it this far into the book, I must warn you: there's no point in carrying on reading if you do not meet the requirement of believing in your ideas. Being a creative person is not only about coming up with good thoughts but being able to sell them to other people too. In most agencies, to make sure your idea sees the light, you must sell it first to your creative partner, then to your Creative Director, then to the client or even to the client's wife who is "the one who knows about these things", as the Marketing Director of a famous brand told me a while back.

The problem is that believing in your ideas is hard. It's not easy. Often, in your own agency you will find people working in opposite directions. How many times have you heard the following statement from one of your colleagues: "I just don't think this is going to please the client." The deadliest sentence ever. A wildcard invented by someone in the accounts department to tell you that in reality, he is the one who decides and that your idea means too much work or effort for him.

Let me tell you something: if you work in an agency where someone uses those words, where someone pretends to be a clairvoyant, where someone thinks they are in the client's mind and guess what they will like or not, I advise you to leave. Don't say anything, do not even give your notice. Don't waste your energy. Just stay in bed and do not go to work because you will never create strong and powerful work if you are surrounded by 'prophets' of the advertising world.

What you need is to work in an agency where they believe in ideas, where the team's main objective is to win an account, or a pitch, instead of going safe to "not lose it". You need a winning mentality in advertising and to think that you know what the client wants is to have a losers' mentality. Unfortunately, 90% of the people that I have worked with fall into the latter category. They fight not to lose an account instead of going for it with all their will.

Funnily enough, those who try not to lose are usually the ones who envy the creatives who do superlative work, and claim that it's only so because the other agency has better clients.

To illustrate better the need to modify your mentality, I would like to share a story that in some way changed my vision and attitude towards clients. As I have already mentioned, I used to work for Buzzman in Paris. At the time, it was known for making a fun campaign about a bear and a hunter for Tipp-Ex. Buzzman was far from an easy place to work in because of the excessive pressure you felt. However, there was something that led them to win more accounts in a couple of years than most agencies in their lifespan. Accounts as important as Burger King, Virgin Mobile, Nivea, Milka, Ikea or Puma. It is especially important that I share with you how they won the Milka (Mondelez) account because it transformed the way I see advertising and clients forever.

At the time, the agency was filled with thirsty creatives led by a guy who absolutely hated making changes based on what the client might prefer. When they entered a pitch for the Milka account, everyone in the agency had the opportunity to contribute with ideas. However, nobody seemed to find anything powerful enough. The agency was betting hard on winning this pitch and looked for creative freelancers who could give a hand. One of them, Miguel Durao, a talented Portuguese copywriter, thought of an idea that amazed the executives of the agency. The idea called "the last square" was as simple as taking a square off the chocolate bar. The last one you eat and, supposedly, the best. On the internet, you had the possibility of getting that last piece back or to send it to someone you loved along with a message.

Although the idea could not be simpler, this involved changing many mechanisms in the way you manufacture and package a Milka chocolate bar. Despite its simplicity, it is exactly the kind of great idea that is usually rejected by your Creative Director/Head of accounts with arguments such as: "it's too complicated", "the customer is not going to get into such a mess", "to win a pitch you need to have a strong concept ", typical killing words that are recurrent in our profession and that I have heard on too many occasions.

Well, luckily, in Buzzman they thought in a diametrically opposite way and they bet all their chips on that one single "crazy" idea. On the day of the presentation, Milka's marketing managers were perplexed when they heard about "the last square" and asked if the agency had any other proposals. They did not have any. After a few moments of silence, Milka's marketing managers asked to be left alone to reflect and think. Upon returning to the room, the marketing director of Milka asked again why they had not brought any more ideas. The creatives of the agency simply replied that they were sure that this idea was the most powerful they had. The marketing director turned to the president of the agency and said: "We do not usually give the answer the same day, but this is a special case. We have loved the idea and we want to do it."

Jubilation took over the agency. They had won Milka's pitch and they had done it by betting on themselves. The campaign took over a year to come to light, but when it did it was a resounding success. In fact, the idea was so popular that the following year, it was executed in 13 countries in the European Union. "The last square" by Milka would also take four lions in Cannes, the Eurobest Grand Prix and an innumerable amount of highly deserved awards.

Beyond the awards, the articles and the pats on the back, the really valuable thing is that the creatives who saw what happened in that agency those weeks changed the way they saw advertising forever. We understood the importance of the words of Jean Anouilh: "Believe in your idea and be willing to die for it."

Therefore, do not let people beat you to a pulp with things such as "the client will want this or the client will want that". If you ever hear that coming out of a boss in your agency, just escape and never look back.

It's the best thing you can do for you.

~

Chapter 22

DON'T COMPETE, JUST WIN.

> "He who knows how to win in victory is twice victorious."
> **Publio Siro**

I remember the feedback I once received from a student of Miami Ad School. She said that "my ego was bigger than all the Miami Ad Schools in the world combined". Initially, I took that comment very badly, because I didn't think it was true. Then it occurred to me that in fact, it might even have been something positive. Maybe she saw me as the typical successful creative guy who walks around like Jack the Lad thinking a few Lions have made him a better person. If only she knew the insecurities that come with being a creative professional! In any case, I suppose that each person will have a different opinion of me, although whoever said that, if you are reading this book, I just want to thank you because your comment inspired me to write this chapter. From the bottom of my heart, thanks a million.

So, ego, ego and more ego. No matter how much you remind creatives to leave their ego at the door of the agency, they always act as if that doesn't apply to them. What is it about our ego? How often do you feel forced to smile and comment positively on the work of one of your colleagues even though you are fuming inside? You are struck by a feeling of hate and unhealthy envy that comes from just how good the work in front of you actually is. That's because each and every one of us wants to win. We want to be the person that everyone admires, with whom everyone wants to work, the advertising God who always has a breakthrough idea, the special one, the most talented person to work with on Earth, or at least in our agency.

However, pretending that you can be this godlike figure for long is absolutely impossible, because every day there will be a new brief and a new opportunity for you to shine but also for your colleagues to shine and steal your moment. Even if you are the daddy of the agency, there will always be other creatives at other workplaces coming up with amazing work that will make you feel that you are not good enough for this job. And that's the issue about being creative. You think that your ideas are synonymous with your worth as a person. If your idea is great, you think you are great. If this week, your colleague has a better idea than yours, then you also think he's better than you as a person. If your idea is trash, you feel like a bum. If your boss tells you that your idea is crap, you feel like crap. If you are a creative nobody, you are a nobody in general.

Your mind is so hard on you that failure in a brief sometimes leads you to rethink your entire life. We don't seem to be able to separate the value of our ideas from our worth as a person. That is the kind of stress that we are subjected to as creatives.

In other types of industries, you can afford a bad day. For example, you may be working in the hospitality industry (I did), and have a bad day. For some reason, you can't be bothered to be as nice with your guests as you should. The good thing is, that you can go home, return the next day a little rejuvenated, and be a better version of yourself and that's it. No one will bother you about your mood swings that much.

What I want to say is that in most industries (and I'm not saying all of them), what is required of you is an acceptable job. In advertising, any brief or request that you receive from a client or creative director involves an unspoken agreement that your work has to be amazing. If you have produced three great campaigns in a row, you still cannot relax. You will still be required to come up with outstanding work for your new client.

One day, you are celebrating, you are getting pat on the back by your boss, the following week he may call you into his office to remind that your work is not up to scratch. So, you end up living in this eternal conflict, asking yourself, "am I good enough or am I not good enough?"

All this tension and conflict that you are living with leads to an almost unavoidable feeling of needing to win all the time. I mean it. Always. At all costs. You need to be the best. The most valued creative of your agency, or the agency network.

I know it sounds bad to say that but in this industry, if you do not feel that burning desire to win and rejoice in victory, to show-off your awards with pride, to make a bit of fun of whomever has not won anything, you may not have the winning spirit that a creative need. A spirit that, I'm afraid, is the only one that can truly distance you from mediocre work and take you to the top.

If you are not an egocentric creative, you may live a happier life, but I doubt your work will reach the levels of excellence that you see out there. I guess both personalities have some good and bad. Producing an amazing campaign and winning awards gives you the joy of a job well done. It might make you earn a little more, receive a better job, have more opportunities. It makes you feel that the struggles and sleepless nights have been worth it. On the other hand, that effort to win separates you from your partner, family and friends.

If you're not careful, like me, you may even start getting anxiety issues. Some people I know have ended up in hospital at the age of 35. I have seen colleagues suffering from panic attacks, psoriasis, depression, extreme stress, chronic migraines, alopecia areata, etc… All due that burning desire to win, to make the best campaign, to feed your ego, and hopefully to win that golden kitten called a Cannes lion that after all your suffering you still need to pay for if you want to keep a copy.

These thoughts are not intended to encourage or discourage anyone. They are a mere observation of what I have lived as a creative. What I have often felt in my gut. I am a bastard who always wants to be placed above others and, therefore that makes me a pretty valuable creative.

Don't misunderstand me, there's only one reason I've won awards at Cannes, One Show, Eurobest, D&AD, etc. It's simply because I was obsessed with the idea of winning. For years, it was the only thing that mattered to me. The obsession that made me go crazy when I saw others winning and I didn't, thinking when will it happen to me?

Again, I do not want to convert anyone into something they are not, but from my experience, I know that if you have that obsession to win, you will do. If you do not have it, you may want to consider if advertising is the right industry for you or pay someone to put that "obsessive about winning" hormone in your body.

~

Chapter 23

No one tests your idea better than YOU.

Mark Twain

In the wonderful world of advertising there is something even more annoying than the aforementioned office 'clairvoyants' or 'prophets' that go about telling you what a client will or will not like. Yes, I'm talking about advertising research. Those tests in which a small fraction of the population sit down to see your campaign (in some, often hastily prepared, form) and determine if that campaign deserves to see the light or if it should be sent to the idea cemetery.

How can an idea that comes from the depths of your very being, which sometimes has no explanation but is simply a marvel of ingenuity and creativity, can be judged in such a cold calculating way as research?

For those who don't know them, the advertising pre-tests intend to evaluate if the proposed campaign will be effective and meet the objectives for which the campaign has been designed. These are some of the guesses that are carried out during a test:

— To 'guess' the acceptance or rejection that a concept or idea provokes.

— To 'guess' if the idea is sufficiently understandable, and if it has potential to leave a lasting impression on customers.

— To 'guess' the level of credibility of the message.
(If this point was to be taken seriously, a great number of campaigns would completely lose the bit of creativity you see in them.
The ads by Skittles, which are known for their surrealistic creativity would have never seen the light).

— To 'guess' the degree of association between the product, the brand, and the advertising message.

— Finally, to 'guess' if the message motivates the purchase and consumption. (I mean seriously, a group of people taking notes can know that?)

This is just a shortlist of some of the parameters. There are many more, but I'd rather move on because this is upsetting me so much. I just find it so dumb that sometimes those investigations that seem so essential for your client, are carried out by groups of as little as five people. Five people with nothing to do all day and that have no idea about marketing or advertising but who are given the power to choose the future of your campaign.

In the face of such castrating moves, there is only one solution: revolution. Dear friends, if you ever set up an advertising agency, please remember the damage you do to creativity if you evaluate your campaigns through these highly robotic procedures.

That what comes out of the right hemisphere of your brain, the creative, the artistic, should not be undone by the left hemisphere of four Muppets who know less about advertising than I did when I did the Spanair print ad I showed at the beginning of this book.

Clench your teeth and defend your idea! If you think it's worth it, defend it.

Your idea is worth it if you jumped when you came up with it.

Your idea is worth it if you had the guts to share it with your partner.

Your idea is worth it if you shared it with another creative person and saw their envy.

Your idea is worth it, if after the initial rush, you still believe in the idea on day 22 as much as you did on day 2.

Your idea is worth it if you wake up the next morning and cannot wait to present it to your creative director.

Your idea is worth it if the creative director gives you his or her approval.

Your idea is worth it if the creative director does not give you his approval but you still feel the need to fight for it.

Your idea is worth it if the client decides to test it again and again.

Your idea is worth it despite what the research Muppets might say.

Your idea is worth it especially if they say something bad about it.

And what if your idea is killed by a test? Then pat yourself on the back, my friend, because it means that your idea was probably f****** good. So, test, test, and test again but whatever happens, whatever the results of these farces, continue believing in your ideas. Don't fall in love with them, but defend them with common sense, because I know when they are worth it, whatever a test might say.

~

Chapter 24

YOU'RE CUPID, STUPID.

> "We are all born for love.
> It is the principle of existence,
> and its only end."
> **Benjamin Disraeli**

Over the course of the last year, I have watched two of my creative students become inseparable. A boy and a girl who did not know each other when they got to Miami Ad School, but after a year of sharing lessons, they were cuddling in my class, completely absorbed in one another and totally ignoring the secrets of the advertising world I was sharing with them.

I wasn't upset about their lack of attention. Something inside of me was grateful as this lovely couple made me realize something that I would not have thought otherwise. Thanks to them I had just discovered what it really means to be a creative: a creative is a real version of Cupid.

We should not just be the people within the agency with an over-inflated ego and our feet up on the table. Nor should we be the just the people that enlighten others with our genius.

Although this is usually a good enough description of what it means to be a creative, I think a better description is that of the creative Cupid, making consumers fall in love with our clients' products and brands through an arrow of creativity. An arrow that we should try to aim well enough for that love story to be as long-lasting as possible. As Luis Bassat said in his "Red Book of Advertising", our industry "puts product and consumer in contact".

When I say Cupid, I'm not asking you to read poems, become experts in solving relationship issues or be a guru of the pick-up game. No, no. My intention is simply that you see your client with different eyes. Your client is not trying to deceive anyone with his positive messages. He should not be considered a liar who goes around thinking only about filling his wallet. He is just a lost person who is desperately looking for a way to make people fall in love with him, and that is somehow quite noble.

Have you never tried to convince a boy or a girl that you would love them forever, with beautiful embellished Shakespearean words? Of course, you have. Well, maybe not with Shakespeare's poems, but possibly with the cheesy lyrics of your current pop idol. We've all done it, with more or less talent, and with more or less fortune. Advertising is the same. It is only a declaration of love that sometimes hits the sweet spot, and sometimes doesn't.

When you look at things this way, you realize that it's not possible to always find the magic needed to make a consumer fall in love with a brand, just as it is impossible for every man to make Julia Roberts fall in love with you. The reality is that no matter how hard you try, if you are not what she wants, there is nothing that will change her opinion.

A person who always drinks Coca-Cola will not start drinking Seven-Up because the brand releases the coolest ad of the year. Coca-Cola simply owns the heart of its audience and you will not tear them apart with some magic advertising tricks. But in case someone tries, Coca-Cola puts constant effort into reminding its consumers of how important they are to the Coca-Cola family. This way, emotions between a consumer and a brand become like that of a couple in the real world.

And that's why our job as creatives is so difficult. Almost impossible. Because our duty is like breaking couples up. We need to steal an audience who cherishes a brand or a product and we have to convince them that this other brand they have used for years is not in reality that good for them. So, in the face of such difficulty, what should we do?

The first step would be to understand your client just as much as you try to understand the final consumers. Too often, in meetings, you are confronted with the embarrassment of not knowing either.

So, on the one hand, it is essential to know your client well: what they like, what they expect from you and your campaign, and what you can contribute to their organization. If you listen carefully, at some stage they will also drop a comment that you can use to feed their ego. Use it to make him believe that the campaign idea came from him. If you do that, the chances of getting your campaign produced will grow exponentially.

On the other hand, you must know your consumer. They are even more difficult to please, because they have already been interrupted hundreds of times by advertising campaigns from clients like yours.

So, to make both fall in love, it is vital to find a nexus that both appreciate. There is no methodology for that except to try to genuinely know who you are talking to. Study them, follow them everywhere, get to know everything about them, and when you do, you will only need to notch an arrow and let it fly. Time to think of new ideas Cupid!

~

Chapter 25

Make the HEADLINES with your HEADLINES.

> "The first sentence of a book is a handshake, perhaps an embrace."
> **Jhumpa Lahiri**

The world of advertising is changing and is becoming more and more visual. Gone are the days of Madmen when the copywriter was the king and the art director a simple Muppet "used" to make a visual of the copywriter's idea.

Art directors have now taken over. In fact, as teacher, I am amazed at the number of teams composed of two art directors who share the writing between them. This might be the reason for tall the abominable headlines out there.

It is a pity that the role of copywriter is diminishing when, with the use of a smart headline, a brilliant and award-worthy campaign can be created.

I remember my former creative director at Y&R Prague, who in just over six years, went from being a senior creative to a European Chief Creative Officer. He always told people in the agency: "If I had to give advice to a creative, I would tell him or her to learn to write good headlines".

Considering that a few of us still think that copywriting is important, I feel obliged to share with you a small study that I have conducted about the art of writing headlines. All of it from the perspective of someone who takes note of the recommendations that 'experts' have been giving for years and years. And years.

Experts have always told me:

"Do not use questions in the tagline."

Yes, it's true, it's not very common. But it is also true that one of the most famous taglines in the history of advertising is "Got milk?" Created by Goodby, Silverstein and Partners. This is not only a question, but a grammatically incorrect one at that. Conclusion: ask questions if you want.

Experts have always told me:

"Exaggerations are the worst thing you can do in the whole advertising universe."

Perhaps, but it is also true that the most famous copy campaigns in the world are undoubtedly those of the magazine 'The Economist, of which 90% are huge exaggerations about the intelligence and financial ability of their readers. Conclusion: exaggerate if you want.

MAKE THE HEADLINES WITH YOUR HEADLINES

Image 32

Experts have always told me:

"Do not use abbreviations or acronyms."

As you have already noticed, I do not like to contradict the experts, but the truth is that I have seen more than one campaign that uses acronyms to get the attention of the viewer. The first one that comes to my mind is a fun print campaign for the TV series 'Unbreakable Kimmy Schmidt' (Image 32).

In this specific case, the acronyms get your attention because you know what they should refer to (something that the audience assumes would never be able to run) and instead they refer to something totally different.

When you see MILF, you think of "Mum I'd like to f***". That gets your attention. But when you read the ad closely, MILF stands for "My interesting lady friend".

In another execution in this series, "STFU" which we read as "Shut the f*** up" is reinterpreted as "Save the flying unicorns".

The twist of these acronyms is a funny deception, which in my opinion, fulfills its purpose of getting people's attention. Conclusion: use acronyms if you want.

Experts have always told me:

"**Comparisons are worse than clichés.**"

Maybe, but there are also numerous cases in which a comparative structure helps you convey a clear and powerful message. For example, in this Movistar print ad, to make people aware of the dangers of using a mobile phone while driving, the creatives decided to make a comparison between driving while using a phone, and driving on an obviously perilous road (Image 33). The campaign shows some of the most dangerous road in the world, but the headlines explain, "The road you take to the movies is more dangerous than this one." A comparison that seems untrue, until you read the subhead, "When you use a mobile phone while driving."

Image 33

Conclusion: Make comparisons if you want.

Well, you probably think that I am a rebel or a stubborn man who enjoys finding exceptions to rules. In reality though, I am only sharing my opinion, our industry already has plenty of limitations, it's far from us to impose more unnecessarily. If you make an ad, there are a lot of things that you are never going to be able to say. Let's not make it harder than it already is.

I reiterate the advice I gave in chapter 20. When you write headlines, you should only have one thing in mind: get your audience's attention, create curiosity or show the benefit. If your ad meets one of these requirements, you're on track.

I encourage you to write with complete freedom, to forget the rules, so long as you do it well. This is advertising. You will not save the world, even if some of most famous campaigns pretend they do. Just write with passion and let your words flow. The important thing is that you free your mind and you let those fingers do the talking.

~

Chapter 26

THE
END.

THE END

Charles Bukowski

Yes, all the stories come to an end. And this is the end of my book. My first book. Maybe the first of many, or maybe the last. The truth is that I do not know. I prefer not to know. What difference does it make, anyway? I had a good time writing it. And I hope you enjoyed it too.

I have written it in the most honest and generous way I could. Trying to share with you all the knowledge that I have accumulated in these years working in advertising.

Some will agree with many of the things I have shared, others will deny everything. The world of advertising is like that. There's little you can do about it. Even the sales of this book will not determine whether it is good or not. It may be bought by thousands of people and adored all over the world or it may be bought by a handful of people who will consider it a piece of junk. It may even be added to a pile of old books at an advertising agency. The kind of pile everyone likes to have to rest their feet on, and even though all the creatives there have agreed that the book is worthless, in a moment of no inspiration, they will decide to take a quick look to see if they can save the brief and impress their creative director.

No, ladies and gentlemen, God did not make me creative nor did he make me a mind-reader. The truth is that I'm not sure what he made me. The only thing I know is my past and my present and how I went from delivering pizzas, to working in construction, to being a character in Disney, to working in the hotel trade, to being a creative, then a lecturer, and now an author. And, who knows what else I will do in the future?

Whatever route I take, I hope to continue working in the world of advertising. I hope to make honest campaigns that reach and touch people, without the need to think that advertising can change the world. I hope this industry evolves in a way that allows everyone to get paid justly for their enormous efforts, whether they are a trainee or the general manager of an agency. I hope that everyone, after reading this book will feel capable of becoming a better creative. I hope this book makes you feel that it's possible, because it really is. I hope that one day I will look back and feel that this book has been inspiring and of some value for you.

THE END

Time will tell. And although everything in this industry is so ephemeral, I will continue to work day in day out with passion and desire, and drive advertising crazy just as it has driven me crazy. Like the ad for Atletico de Madrid from Sra. Rushmore said: Advertising "kills me". Advertising "gives me life". If that's how you feel about it too, then I am glad this book fell in your hands. If you don't feel like that yet, I hope I have instigated some curiosity and renewed passion for it.

I am not good at saying goodbye so I'll make this quick: big hugs for each and every one of you. Thanks for reading this book and for continuing to fight for the ideas that make the rest of us want to give a standing ovation.

~

ACKNOWLEDGEMENTS.

ACKNOWLEDGEMENTS

Thank you

In life, when you get something done it is as much for your efforts as for the circumstances and the people who have crossed your path. There are many people who have helped me be here today, and I would like to thank them all.

First, I would like to not only thank but dedicate this book to my family. To my sister for being the only person who always believes in me, even when I am in points of my life where my future promises very little. Thanks for always finding the right words to make me feel special and encourage me to keep going in my adventures, whatever they may be.

To my mother (whom I like to call "Mothereck" or "Mamiki"), who has taken care of me like no one, who has endured my mood swings with heroism, who has always put my comfort before hers and that has instilled values in me to become an honest person that will not cheat you with this book. You have my Mother's word.

To my father, for teaching me countless ways to ignore negative people who sometimes try to meddle in your affairs. I thank you for working hard so that my sister and I did not lack anything.

To Psembi, who I met a in Barcelona a few years back because we worked for the same company. An amazing creative talent with a bright future in advertising. Thanks for helping me out with the English version of this book, which would have never seen the light without you.

To my friends Langas, Pepotas and Raulicas. The most awesome dudes, each in their own way, who welcomed me with open arms when we started working together in advertising a few years ago.

To Ana Hidalgo and Manu Cabanillas, for putting their trust in me and making me a teacher in Miami Ad School. Thanks for allowing me to teach the new generation of publicists.

To my boss in London, Manuel de Brito, who despite losing his daughter and his wife, always had the strength to come to work and teach me to be an educated person with values. An amazing professional and, above all, one of the best people I've ever met.

To Pingüi and Pablo, for giving me my first job in advertising and for always treating me with respect in an industry where respect does not always survive.

To my friend Jorju, I forgot to mention in the original Spanish version of this book. For being my friend for over 20 years, even if it meant having to deal patiently with my swing moods and my edgy personality.

To my friend Héctor, for always being there although our lives have been very different and we have been in little contact for many years. You are still my "Brother".

To my colleague Charlie, who despite being in Paris, always sends good vibes. *"Je t'adore tonton."*

To my ex-partner Atila, for helping me get the best out of me as a creative even though that meant starting to have anxiety problems. With him I discovered the price of winning several Lions. I owe him a few tricks and a couple of chapters of this book.

To my mate Neil, who without a doubt is the best designer I have worked with and who happens to be even fussier than me when it came to illustrating this book. If it looks this good, it is only thanks to your effort and passion.

To all my colleagues who have made me enjoy their company as much as I hope they have enjoyed mine.

And finally, to all those who have hardened me with sticks. I do not thank them. I prefer to send them a good smack.

~

Glossary

Brief*:
Document confirming understanding between a client and an advertising agency on objectives of an advertising campaign, identification of the targeted audience, strategies to be adopted in reaching the audience, the timeframe of the campaign, and its total estimated cost.

Brainstorming*:
Process for generating creative ideas and solutions through intensive and freewheeling group discussion. Every participant is encouraged to think aloud and suggest as many ideas as possible, no matter seemingly how outlandish or bizarre. Analysis, discussion, or criticism of the aired ideas is allowed only when the brainstorming session is over and evaluation session begins. See also lateral thinking and nominal group technique.

Target Group:
Segment of people to whom an advertising campaign is directed.

Tagline:
A sentence that expresses the purpose of a brand and / or its value proposition.

Case study:
Video summary of an advertising campaign that is usually done to sell your idea to the jury of an award festival.

Shortlist:
List of campaigns that have been selected as finalists in an advertising festival.

Big Data:
Term that is used to talk about the analysis of large volumes of data that brands use in advertising to ensure the effectiveness of their marketing strategies.

Scam ad:
Campaign created and paid for by an advertising agency, usually with the permission of a brand, to present it to advertising festivals in order to win an award.

*http://www.businessdictionary.com/

Credits

Brand: Volvo.
Campaign: Interception.
Agency: Grey, New York.

Brand: Burger King.
Campaign: McWhopper.
Agency: Y&R, New Zealand.

Brand: Unicef.
Campaign: Close Unicef.
Agency: JWT, Madrid.

Brand: Giovanni Rana.
Campaign: The First Website you can eat.
Agency: Remo, Madrid.

Brand: ING Direct.
Campaign: Cómete nuestra web.
Agency: JWT, Madrid.

Brand: Acierto.Com.
Campaign: Hand.
Agency: Remo, Madrid.

Brand: Arsys.
Campaña: Hello Juan!
Agency: Remo, Madrid.

Brand: Norwegian Airlines.
Campaign: Brad is single.
Agency: Marketing department.

Brand: Animal.
Campaign: Trumpdonald.org.
Agency: Animal, Stockholm.

Brand: Scotch (Student work)
Campaign: Scotchland.
Agency: A creative team from France.

Brand: Kit-Kat.
Campaign: Have a Break. Brexit.
Agency: Chris Smallwood

Brand: Liberty Mutual.
Campaign: Heidi Kloser.
Agency: Havas Worldwide.

Brand: Vodafone.
Campaign: Double Back.
Agency: Colenso BBDO, Auckland.

Brand Liberty Mutual.
Campaign: Heidi Kloser.
Agency: Havas Worldwide.

Brand: Marmite.
Campaign: Love it or Hate it.
Agency: DDB, London.

Brand: Yorkie.
Campaign: It's not for girls.
Agency: JWT, London.

Brand: Hans Brinker hotel.
Campaign: Accidentally Eco-friendly.
Agency: Kesselskramer, Amsterdam.

Brand: Familiprix.
Campaign: Knife, Skateboard, Headache.
Agency: Bos, Canada.

Brand: 11811.
Campaign: Baby.
Agency: Pingüino Torreblanca, Madrid.

Brand: Acierto.com.
Campaign: Boomerang.
Agency: Remo, Madrid.

Brand: Ssangyong.
Campaign: Beethoven.
Agency: Pingüino Torreblanca, Madrid.

Brand: Siemens.
Campaign: The appliance brand that starts with 'Yes'.
Agency: Remo, Madrid.

Brand: Danonino.
Campaign: Say yes.
Agency: Y&R, Barcelona.

Brand: Harvey-Nichols.
Campaign: Sorry, I spent it on myself.
Agency: Adam&Eve DDB, London.

Brand: Dove.
Campaign: Camera Shy.
Agency: Ogilvy, London.

Brand: Atlético de Madrid.
Campaign: Me mata. Me da la vida.
Agency: Sra Rushmore, Madrid.

Brand: Harley-Davidson.
Campaign: A piece of Freedom.
Agency: Y&R, Prague.

Brand: Crisis Relief.
Campaign: Liking isn't helping.
Agency: Publicis, Singapore.

Brand: Freddo.
Campaign: Falls.
Agency: Y&R, Sao Paulo.

Brand: Sunlight.
Campaign: Separate them (Pig).
Agency: Lowe, Bangkok.

Brand: VW.
Campaign: Fun theory.
Agency: DDB, Stockholm.

Brand: The Pilion trust charity.
Campaign: Fuck the Poor.
Agency: Publicis, London.

Brand: Rethink Homelessness
Campaign: Rethink.
Agency: Rethink Homelessness, Orlando.

Brand: Arrels Foundation.
Campaign: Homeless fonts.
Agency: The Cyranos/McCann, Barcelona.

Brand: Recife FC.
Campaign: Immortal fans.
Agency: Ogilvy, Brazil.

Brand: Recife FC.
Campaign: Security Moms.
Agency: Ogilvy, Brazil.

Brand: Tipp-ex.
Campaign: The Social Book.
Agency: Buzzman, Paris.

Brand: Dove.
Campaign: Real Beauty Sketches.
Agency: Ogilvy, Brazil.

Brand: No somos delito.
Campaign: Holograms for freedom.
Agency: DDB, Madrid.

Brand: Intermarché.
Campaign: Inglorious fruits & vegetables.
Agency: Marcel, Paris.

Brand: States United to Prevent Gun Violence.
Campaign: The Gun shop.
Agency: Grey, New York.

Brand: 350 Action.
Campaign: Climate Name Change.
Agency: Barton F. Graf 9000, New York.

CREDITS

Brand: Volvo.
Campaign: Lifepaint.
Agency: Grey, London.

Brand: Transport Accident Commission.
Campaign: Meet Graham.
Agency: Clemenger BBDO, Melbourne.

Brand: Burger King.
Campaign: Scariest BK.
Agency: David The Agency, Miami.

Brand: Burger King.
Campaign: McWhopper.
Agency: Y&R, New Zealand.

Brand: Samsung.
Campaign: Safety Truck.
Agency: Leo Burnett, Buenos Aires.

Brand: Fundación Favaloro.
Campaign: The salt you can see.
Agency: Grey, Buenos Aires.

Brand: Intermarché.
Campaign: The freshest orange juice.
Agency: Marcel, Paris.

Brand: Teatro Neu.
Campaign: Pay Per Laugh.
Agency: The Cyranos/McCann, Barcelona.

Brand: Walmart.
Campaign: Price on the jersey.
Agency: DM9DDB, Sao Paulo.

Brand: Cancer patients aid association.
Campaign: Smoking cures cancer.
Agency: Ogilvy & Mather, Mumbai.

Brand: The Economist.
Campaign: Management trainee.
Agency: Abbott, London.

Brand: De Beers.
Campaign: Headache.
Agency: JWT, New York.

Brand: MACMA.
Campaign: Man Boobs for Boobs.
Agency: David the Agency, Miami.

Brand: Milka.
Campaign: The last square.
Agency: Buzzman, Paris.

Brand: Milk.
Campaign: Got milk?
Agency: Goodby Silverstein and Partners, San Francisco.

Brand: Unbreakable Kimmy Schmidt.
Campaign: DTF, MILF, STFU.
Agency: Darewin.

Brand: Movistar.
Campaign: If you text and drive.
Agency: Y&R, Lima.

NOTES

www.ingramcontent.com/pod-product-compliance
Lightning Source LLC
Chambersburg PA
CBHW051306220526
45468CB00004B/1232